EXPLAINING
REFORM
JUDAISM

EXPLAINING REFORM JUDAISM

Eugene B. Borowitz
and Naomi Patz

BEHRMAN HOUSE, INC., PUBLISHERS

Book Designer: Gilda Hannah

© Copyright 1985 by Eugene B. Borowitz and Naomi Patz
Published by Behrman House, Inc.
235 Watchung Avenue
West Orange, N.J. 07052

Manufactured in the United States of America
4 5 6 7 8 9 10

Library of Congress Cataloging in Publication Data

Borowitz, Eugene B., Naomi Patz
  Explaining Reform Judaism.

  Summary: Presents the history and theology of the
Reform movement in Judaism.
    1. Reform Judaism—Juvenile literature. [1. Reform
Judaism] I. Patz, Naomi. II. Title.
BM197.B655   1985   296.8′346   85-3998
ISBN 0-87441-394-X

For Norman, Debby and Aviva
for all the reasons they know

and

For all Reform rabbis and children
in Reform religious schools for all
the Jewish hopes they represent

Contents

PART ONE

What Makes Reform Jews Special?

By all rights, Judaism should have disappeared two thousand years ago after the Romans destroyed its center, the Temple in Jerusalem. Yet our religion and our people are still strong today. Why?

In those days, the Pharisees created new ways to keep Judaism alive. They taught that our religion need not depend upon priests and sacrifices. Instead, they called for synagogues, study and the performance of *mitzvot* by every Jew. This dramatically changed the Jewish way of life.

In the last two hundred years, Jews have also had to develop changes to meet the challenge of democracy. The experiments in living as modern Jews that we call Reform Judaism brought about many changes in Jewish life—for all Jews.

Why did the first Reformers decide that they needed to make revolutionary changes in Judaism? What new Jewish ideas and ceremonies did they create? And now, two hundred years after it began, how has the Reform movement itself changed?

With these questions we start our exploration of Reform Judaism.

CHAPTER ONE

A New Movement Modernizes Judaism

Almost everything you do would have been illegal for young Jews living in Europe until about two hundred years ago. From 313 C.E. on, European Jews were treated as separate and inferior. They weren't allowed to own land. They weren't allowed in the universities. They couldn't choose where to live. After 1500 C.E., the Jewish neighborhoods became walled ghettos.

In some places Jews had to wear special red or yellow cloth badges, or peculiar "Jews' hats." They could engage only in the few kinds of business that non-Jews thought degrading or particularly unprofitable. Some Jews lent money for interest. Others sold old furniture and used clothing. The guilds that controlled the crafts and trade were closed to Jews. And they could not become apprentices to most of the developing professions, like law and medicine.

Oppressed Outside, They Turn Inward

Jews put up with this because they had no choice. They organized their lives around their dealings with other Jews. They lived by the Jewish calendar, ob-

For hundreds of years the Jews of Europe were forced to live in crowded ghettos, such as this one in the city of Frankfurt, Germany. At night the gates were locked, and no one could go in or out.

served traditional Jewish law and settled their disputes before Jewish courts. They got their education in Jewish schools studying Jewish books. They even spoke their own Jewish language, Yiddish, a sort of Hebrew-German. After a while, it seemed wrong to them to have much contact with Christians. The world outside the Jewish "quarter" (the neighborhood that later became a ghetto) was strange and frightening, to be entered only at one's peril.

This negative picture of Jewish life is oversimplified. There were always some business and cultural exchanges between Jews and gentiles and some countries which were hospitable to Jews. But there were also many forced conversions, murders, pogroms, and outbreaks of violence. Until the end of the eighteenth century (about the time of the American Revolution), most European Jews felt like complete outsiders.

A Revolution in Society and People's Ideas About It

As the 1700s came to an end, there was a radical shift in European politics. People insisted on helping to run their own government—and they cared enough to fight for it. With the French Revolution, in 1789, unprecedented ideas about citizenship came into being.

The Revolution gave "everyone" in France the right to vote, the right to own property, the right to live wherever they chose, the right to work at whatever they wanted, and the opportunity to get an education. But did this include French Jews? No one had really thought about letting Jews become citizens. However, once the Revolution was successful its leaders had to face the logic of their ideas of equality. Universal rights obviously had to mean

Jews were required to wear special identifying marks such as the circular badges shown in this detail from a synagogue stained glass window.

Auwai! es is ken Profitgen dran
Es hat doch wenig Werth mehr.

Before the Emancipation, Jews were allowed to work only in undesirable trades such as cloth-dealing and money-lending. According to the caption in this German caricature, the peddler is complaining because he is unable to support himself from his work.

rights for *everyone*, "even" Jews. The French revolutionaries extended citizenship rights to the Jews, although it took more than three years before they did it. As a result, in later years, whenever Napoleon's army took a city, they destroyed the walls around its ghettos. The idea of equality spread everywhere that people heard about French democracy.

Jewish Responses to the New Opportunity

Historians call the process by which the Jews won citizenship rights—in France and then elsewhere—the Emancipation. Most Jews didn't rush to take advantage of the Emancipation. They were too afraid of the "outside world." The leaders of the German Jewish community were terrified of what the Emancipation might bring. Jews who learned the German language would have too many contacts with Christians and might be lured away from Judaism. So they refused to change the old ghetto-style Jewish ways. Ironically, their insistence that Judaism could not adapt to modern times drove many

Jews to convert to Christianity. The converts felt that one could be *either* modern or Jewish—but not *both* at the same time. For them, giving up Judaism was a small price to pay for the advantages they would gain from full participation in general society.

The Beginning of Reform

Some Jews disagreed with both the Jewish community leadership and with those who were converting to Christianity. They, too, thought that certain Jewish customs had become old-fashioned. But they suggested a new way of dealing with the problem. If Jews used modern culture to make Judaism more beautiful and meaningful, Jews wouldn't need to become Christian in order to be modern. They called their experiments in bringing Judaism up-to-date "Reform" because they were reforming ghetto Judaism to fit a free, modern society.

The first Reformers were not rabbis but merchants. They felt the need to change Judaism most strongly since they were in contact with the Christian community and saw the exciting world now opening to all Jews.

A banker named Israel Jacobson was the most important of these early Reformers. He wanted to see German Jews ready to live as citizens as soon as they got their rights. The ghetto schools didn't teach math, science, or languages. There was no career preparation. So in 1801, Israel Jacobson started a modern Jewish school (at his own expense) in Seesen, the town where he lived.

This school was radical for its day. For the first time Jewish boys and girls were taught together. Most girls had never received any formal education. Their mothers taught them how to keep a good Jewish home and, perhaps, how to work in the family business. But they didn't go to school. Jacobson, like the other Reformers, took the idea of equality very seriously and applied it to male and female Jews alike, thus beginning the long struggle for women's equality in Judaism.

Jacobson also changed the traditional *yeshivah* curriculum. His pupils were taught secular subjects like arithmetic, science, and the German language. Most shocking of all, when Christian parents asked to have their children admitted to Jacobson's school, he gladly accepted them. He not only wanted Jews to get along with their Christian neighbors, he wanted at least some Christians to know and respect their Jewish neighbors too.

Of course Jacobson's school taught the Jewish religion—but in an unexpected way. Jacobson insisted that Judaism be taught with the same modern educational techniques used to teach other subjects. He wanted Judaism studied in an orderly, logical fashion. His idea helped to stimulate the modern rethinking of Judaism.

The Most Radical Reform: Beautifying Services

In the long run, nothing was more important than what happened at the weekly religious service in the school's "Temple," which was dedicated in 1810.

The service at Jacobson's school was very different from the normal pattern in the synagogue. It was well organized, orderly, and dignified—the Western European idea of what was beautiful and solemn. The decorum of most other Jewish services in Germany was an Eastern European one. While from time to time the cantor would chant a prayer, the worshipers were generally on their own, causing a hubbub. The service was so long that some people would "take a break" in the middle and others would come in very late—and begin at the beginning. In addition, because the cantor repeated certain prayers, there were usually many side conversations. This Eastern informality was embarrassing to the modernized Jews.

Jacobson shortened the service, mostly by omitting the repetitions. Many prayers were translated into German so the worshipers could understand what they were praying. People were expected to arrive on time, participate in unison, and be solemn and respectful at all times.

The Reformers also borrowed some of the church practices they considered most beautiful. Chief among these were the use of an organ and a "mixed" choir (men and women singing together—another early effort at

Israel Jacobson was the "father of Reform Judaism." His new programs modernized worship services, gave women an active role in religious life, and helped Jews cope with being both Jewish and modern.

Organ music was a prominent feature in the new Reform congregations. Since traditional congregations did not use musical instruments, many people were horrified by this change, seeing in it an adaptation of church practices for synagogue use. The synagogue in this picture is the Lindenstrasse, in Berlin.

equality). Since only men sang at traditional Jewish services, these innovations opened a whole new direction for synagogue music.

Another practice Reformers borrowed was the sermon. Until this time, only a few sermons, in Yiddish and Hebrew, were preached at Jewish services, mostly before major holidays to remind people about particular rituals. At the new Reform temples, the sermons discussed the problems Jews faced every day, and because these sermons were in German the whole congregation could understand what was said.

Many adults found these changes so appealing that they began worshiping together with Jacobson's students at the weekly service.

By 1817 it was time for another creative step. People had accepted the idea of a whole class of young men (not just a single boy, as at the usual Bar Mitzvah ceremony) standing before the congregation to proclaim loyalty to Judaism and to their country (a very new idea in itself). Reformers in Berlin argued that since young women were being educated with the young men, they should be confirmed with them as well. They should formally be welcomed as worshipers and leaders in the synagogue ritual. A class composed of girls and boys was confirmed in Berlin in 1817. This innovation made such sense that in the following year, girls were confirmed with boys in the Hamburg congregation too.

These changes—and the very idea of daring to change—provoked great controversy in Jewish communities all over Germany, as we shall now see.

CHAPTER TWO

A Revolutionary Idea

*L*eopold Zunz was a young scholar—not a rabbi—interested in teaching about Judaism. He often gave the sermon at the Reform service in the Berlin mansion of Jacob Herz Beer. Zunz and the others who preached there talked a lot about the new spirit of freedom in the country. They urged the worshipers to combine Judaism with the new ideas being published in German magazines and books. The service itself gave them a weekly example of how Jewish content could be in harmony with modern German cultural styles.

Many people were excited by these reforming ideas. This alarmed the official leaders of the Berlin Jewish community. They were afraid that the experiments in the Beer Temple would pull too many Jews away from traditional practice or even lead Jews to convert to Christianity. They were so upset that they broke an old, important Jewish "rule." Instead of keeping it "in the Jewish family," they made a formal complaint to the Prussian government about the sermons at the Reform Temple. Since there was no separation of religion and state in Prussia, that meant calling in the police.

After the French Revolution, many governments feared that they would lose control if they gave people even a little freedom. Besides, they believed strongly that Christianity was the only true religion. An old-fashioned, out-of-date and disappearing Judaism served their needs better than an adaptable forward-looking one.

So for different, almost opposite reasons, both the Jewish and the state governmental authorities condemned the sermons. They said that preaching wasn't a Jewish thing to do, that since it had never been a regular part of the Jewish service, it had no place in a Jewish service now.

In 1823, the king of Prussia issued an order which said that Jewish religious services must be held only in existing synagogues. This meant that no new synagogues would be allowed, and services like the one at the Beer Temple in Berlin were illegal. Furthermore, the king decreed that only the traditional ritual could be followed. No changes whatsoever could be made in language, customs, prayers, or songs which were "in accordance with the ancient custom." In other words, sermons and all other reforms were forbidden by law.

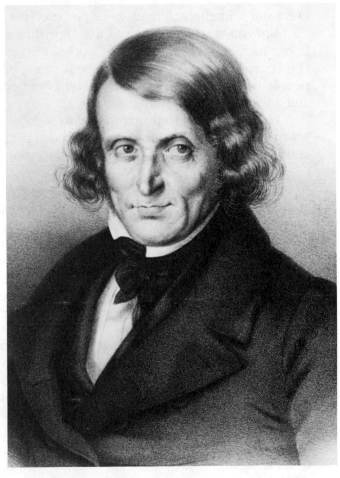

Using university methods of scholarship, Leopold Zunz proved that regular sermons were actually an old and honored Jewish tradition. His discovery was an extremely important contribution to the cause of post-Emancipation Judaism.

How Do You Know What's Jewish?

Leopold Zunz was outraged. Anyone can *say* that sermons aren't Jewish, Zunz reasoned, but how do you *know* it? The answer of the Jewish community leaders was simple: "Our most respected rabbis have said that sermons aren't Jewish. Besides, you don't see them preaching sermons, do you? And neither did our parents' and grandparents' rabbis."

This only made Zunz more stubborn. He wanted to know what *proof* there was of what the "ancient custom" was like. He was too modern to accept traditional statements without evidence. He also needed evidence in order to convince the Prussian government that its order was wrong—that, in fact, giving sermons had long been a Jewish practice. Zunz set out to find proper evidence. He applied the scholarship techniques he had learned in his university studies and created a "scientific" method of studying Judaism. By examining Jewish documents with the same critical thoroughness used in every other intellectual field, Zunz prepared his case.

Midrash was Zunz's key to the "Jewishness" of sermons. The *midrash* books include a vast literature of stories, discussions, and short sayings. The chief purpose of *midrash* seems to be teaching biblical ideas in ways that help people with their own lives. *Midrashim* offer people courage, hope, comfort, and a touch of Jewish holiness.

Zunz was convinced that the *midrash* books contained condensed, old Jewish sermons. He believed they had been preached in ancient synagogues and that Jewish preaching had continued for hundreds of years after the time of the Talmud.

Through exhaustive study of the language and the comments in the *midrash* books, Zunz, after years of study, proved his point. He showed that sermons, preached in whatever language the people spoke, had been an honored and accepted Jewish custom for many centuries.

A Dangerous Precedent

Zunz could now make a strong plea for the modernization of post-ghetto Judaism. He had proof that the governmental authorities who had stopped the experimenters from preaching sermons were preventing them from returning to an ancient, traditional Jewish practice. Although he never actually said so, Zunz made it very clear that the government's real purpose was not to protect Judaism from change but to stop the renewal of a strong Jewish faith. Keeping Judaism from changing would kill it. As Zunz's study of Jewish history showed, Judaism had always changed to meet new conditions. It needed to do so again.

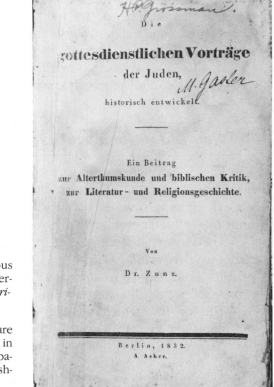

Right: Here is the title page of Zunz's famous work on sermons. Can you read any of the German? The title is best translated as *The Historical Development of the Jewish Sermon.*

Bottom: In a formal procession, Torah scrolls are carried to the dedication of a new synagogue in Memmingen, Bavaria (1913). Note the participation of women in the ceremony, and the fashionable dress of the congregants.

The Prussian government understood the implications of Zunz's book so well that they suppressed his introduction. The introduction called for regular sermons and religious instruction for adults and young people in the vernacular, "in accordance with the ancient tradition."

To this day, we study Jewish sources in Zunz's questioning, historical way—the "scientific" approach known in German as the *wissenschaft* method.

Why Did the Jewish Leaders Fight the Idea of Change?

The Jewish community leaders weren't convinced by Zunz's brilliant discoveries about sermons. These traditionalists were alarmed lest once people started adopting new practices and giving up old ones, they'd keep changing until they weren't even Jewish anymore.

The Jews who were against innovation believed that if something were really true it would last forever. Only wrong ideas or laws have to be improved—and they were sure that their Judaism was perfect. Of course, this sense of certainty also made them feel very safe.

The Jewish teachers of earlier centuries had special reasons for stressing the idea of the permanence of Judaism. After the destruction of the Second Temple (70 C.E.), most Jews were scattered in different countries around the world. They had to adapt to foreign lands and changing times in order to survive in the places where they were permitted to settle. But they also wanted to be good Jews. They felt an enormous need to show that the things they were now doing were really very much what Jews had always done.

This *midrash* about Moses may help explain the Rabbis' attitude: At the time when God told Moses that he was chosen for a special mission, he was given the power to look into the future. He listened to the Rabbinic Court (the Sanhedrin) discussing the Torah. He was amazed to hear all the new laws that Rabbi Akiba discovered in the Torah. "This is not the Torah You gave me," Moses said. "I don't recognize it." Then Moses heard what other Rabbis in the Sanhedrin were saying: "These laws are part of the traditions Moses received on Mount Sinai." When Moses heard this he was no longer upset. He understood that the Rabbis felt they had added nothing new. They only interpreted what was already there. As one talmudic teacher put it, "Whatever a respected scholar introduces in his time was already revealed to Moses when he got the Torah on Mount Sinai."

The Rabbis were not trying to fool themselves or anyone else. When a new problem arose, they looked for precedents in the Torah text or tradition. Then they could feel that they weren't "changing" Judaism but only reexplaining it in terms of their own lives. Most changes actually came about so gradually that no one noticed them. Thus, Judaism was able to grow and develop and yet, at the same time, seem completely unchanged.

Among the benefits of the Emancipation was citizenship, enabling Jews to participate, for the first time, in the civil and political life of their countries. This banquet, in Vienna, Austria, was held in honor of the eightieth birthday of Emperor Franz Joseph I.

Unfortunately, by the eighteenth and nineteenth centuries what had once been a flexible, sensitive system was now rigid. As Jews were liberated from the ghetto and could freely enter society, the issue of change was on everyone's mind. Many people wanted to know how they could live and work outside the ghetto, speak German, dress like their non-Jewish neighbors, get a Western-style high school and college education, and still stay Jewish. The traditionalist leaders of the Jewish community said it was too great a break with the past and couldn't be done. They didn't want to destroy the kind of

Judaism that existed, which they believed stretched right back to the time of Moses or even Abraham.

Historically, they were wrong, as Zunz's method of study showed again and again. The Bar Mitzvah ceremony, for example, hadn't existed earlier than the twelfth century. It is certainly old, but not something that had "always" been part of Judaism. It was once as new to Judaism as the Confirmation ceremony that the traditionalists now found disagreeable. Here is another example: Many Jews had prayed with uncovered heads until well into the Middle Ages. Despite that fact, the *kippah* soon became the basis of huge fights between the traditionalists, who insisted that it be worn, and those Reformers who wanted to pray bareheaded in the Western style.

Leopold Zunz did not start Reform Judaism. Although he was too modern to remain an Orthodox traditionalist, he objected to some of the radical changes and ideas of the early Reform Jews. Other scholars became the intellectual leaders of the movement to modernize Judaism, and ideas other than the modern study of history were critical to them.

Darwin and Reform

Some years after Zunz's book showed that changes had occurred throughout Jewish history, Charles Darwin presented the world with his startling theory of evolution. Darwin said that all animals, including human beings, started from the very simplest forms of life. Over many thousands of years, the simpler life forms changed and evolved into more complex creatures. The theory of evolution not only started a revolution in biology but in people's thinking about all of life. Darwin's theory said that change, not permanence, was natural. What didn't change and adapt to new situations—like dinosaurs—died out. To survive, to flourish, all things needed to evolve.

Darwin's theory strengthened the Reformers' certainty that they were right. Judaism has to change, just as everything else in life must change. The ghetto styles and ghetto answers to old questions could no longer satisfy Jews who wanted to live as equals in the modern world. Rigid inflexibility would kill Judaism. But there was another way. Judaism was strong enough and true enough to evolve forms that would work for modern Jews. If they could create and live these new forms, they would save Judaism.

CHAPTER THREE

Reform Comes to America

Many problems kept the promises of the Emancipation from being fully realized in Europe. Reactionary governments came back into power. They controlled religion and denied freedom. Those people who wanted to resist change could call on the government to help them fight innovation. Liberal synagogues, therefore, had a very difficult time. Although Reform didn't die in Europe, it remained a fragile and somewhat exotic blossom.

America provided the ideal climate for Reform Judaism. American democracy separates religion and state. There has never been any government control of religion here. The entire atmosphere of the country has always encouraged freedom, growth, and change. The synagogues that were established in America did not have to compete with others that already had official state recognition and traditions stretching back for centuries, as in Europe.

The Jews who came to North America, whose very immigration was a big break with the past, brought with them the practices of their European communities. At first, this meant that they and their congregations were rather traditional—but not for very long. They had to adapt their observances to the conditions they found here. Besides, until well into the nineteenth century there were no rabbis or Jewish scholars in America to correct their practices or teach them about their Jewish heritage.

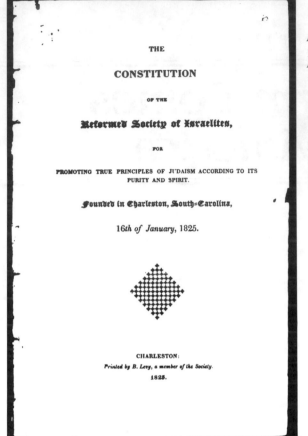

THE

CONSTITUTION

OF THE

Reformed Society of Israelites,

FOR

PROMOTING TRUE PRINCIPLES OF JUDAISM ACCORDING TO ITS
PURITY AND SPIRIT.

Founded in Charleston, South=Carolina,

16th of January, 1825.

CHARLESTON:
Printed by B. Levy, a member of the Society.
1825.

Reform means a continuing process of change and adaptation; *Reformed* has the sense of something already fixed and concluded. Reform Jews today never use the past tense in referring to the name of our movement, although that is the name originally given to the first Reform congregation in the United States, established in Charleston, South Carolina, in 1825.

For all these reasons, the Reformers had an easier time modernizing Judaism in America than they did in Europe. As early as 1824, a group of Jews in Charleston, South Carolina, had their own liberalized service. They soon founded the first Reform congregation in America.

The Two Great Waves of 19th Century Immigrants

The first Jewish settlers arrived in America in the seventeenth century from Spanish and Portuguese speaking countries. In the early nineteenth century, Jews from Western European countries, primarily Germany, sailed to America. They had experienced the Emancipation. Most were modern in their outlook. Many were familiar with the activities of the early Reformers. When Reform rabbis and teachers began coming to America in the 1840s, their ideas were immediately popular with great numbers of Jews.

In 1880 the immigration pattern shifted. Jews from Eastern Europe began to arrive in huge numbers. Eastern European Jews continued to come here in a mass migration until 1924, when United States law drastically cut

The Jewish immigrants from Western Europe were comfortable as both modern Jews and as citizens of the United States. Many of them took part in elegant social events such as this Purim Charity Ball.

Levi Strauss was one of many Jewish peddlers who carried their packs into frontier areas, later opening stores and clothing factories.

immigration. By then, Jews from Eastern Europe had become the Jewish majority in this country. Their background was extremely different from that of Western European Jews. These Jews had not been emancipated. Many of them—like Tevye, in *Fiddler on the Roof*—had no secular education or modern world view. They came from countries where Jews lived in isolation. Many spoke only Yiddish. Once in America, they tended to settle in densely packed neighborhoods in the very largest cities.

The new immigrants were obviously not attuned to German-style Reform Judaism. The Reformers, for their part, were very comfortable with the highly Americanized kind of Judaism they had developed and they—not tra-

The influx of huge numbers of Yiddish-speaking Eastern European Jews created tensions within the established Jewish community. Can you read the Yiddish sign on the vendor's pushcart?

ditionalists—were providing the leadership for the whole American Jewish community. Let's see what their Reform Judaism looked like around the year 1900.

The Style of the Services

Services in Reform congregations were conducted in English, the language of most of the members of the congregation. A majority used the prayer book written by American Reform rabbis, published in 1895. Almost every Reform congregation used an organ, had a choir made up of men and women, and sang English hymns. The services were conducted with great formality and dignity. Sermons, preached every week, often dealt with general human problems as well as with Jewish concerns.

In Europe, most Reform Jews had continued to wear *kippot* at services. This custom followed the old Eastern tradition of keeping heads covered as a sign of respect. In Western countries, on the other hand, it has been considered disrespectful—particularly in the presence of someone important (and who is more important than God?)—for a man to wear a hat indoors. The American Reformers felt that praying bareheaded was the right way to show respect to God. They decided that at their services men should keep their heads uncovered.

Changing More than Styles

The European experiment in shortening the service had now been fully worked out. A number of new changes made the American service shorter still. Over the centuries, many intricate Hebrew poems known as *piyyutim* had been added to the prayer book. Nothing was omitted to make room for them since the rules prohibited dropping any of the regular prayers. Although the *piyyutim* were written in a particularly complicated style, and therefore almost incomprehensible, they were the lyrics of the cantors' most important (and longest) songs. Because they made the service drag on, the Reformers eliminated them.

They also cut out all repetition of prayers. The *tefillah*, or *amidah*, is the central part of the service. In traditional congregations, it is first said quietly by the worshipers and then chanted out loud by the cantor so that people who do not know Hebrew will have this most important group of prayers said for them. The repetition seemed unnecessary now that the Reformers' service was largely in English. It, too, was eliminated.

The Reformers shortened the Shabbat and festival services even further

The Jew on this Torah crown by Ilya Schor "remembers" the Temple destroyed in Jerusalem (pictured as the center of the flower above his head).

This circular calendar dates from fourteenth century Spain. By turning a parchment disk, people could find the dates of Jewish holidays or the names of the weekly Torah readings.

by cutting out a second double recitation of most of these prayers, called *musaf*, the "additional" service. That requires a bit of explanation.

In biblical times, in the Temple, the priests offered a special holiday sacrifice on Shabbat and festivals in *addition* to the daily sacrifice. After the destruction of the Temple, the Rabbis ruled that prayer services would substitute for the Temple sacrifices. (Much of the synagogue service to this day stems from this regulation.) So the Rabbis added a *musaf*, or "additional" set of prayers to each Saturday and festival morning service. The *musaf* service primarily repeats the regular morning *tefillah* (prayers), but adds some passages concerning the sacrifices.

The Reformers rejected the *musaf* service for two reasons. First, it meant reciting many prayers four times in a row. The second reason was that the Reform movement was against sacrifices. Killing animals and then skinning them, pouring their blood out at the altar and finally burning parts or all of them, seemed to these modern Jews no way to pray to God. It was certainly not anything they ever wanted to do themselves. Moreover, some prayers in the *musaf* service speak of our longing to "return" from our exile to the Land of Israel to rebuild the ancient Temple and once again offer sacrifices to God. Now that Jews were free and equal citizens of the country in which they lived, the Reformers felt that prayers which talk of our "exile" and "return" or our "longing for Zion" were out of place. The leader of the Reform congregation in Charleston, South Carolina put it this way at the service dedicating the first American Reform congregation (in 1825): "This country is our Palestine, this city our Jerusalem, this house of God our temple."

This use of the word "temple" was also something new. Until Reform began, the word "Temple" had always meant *the* Temple in Jerusalem, the one commanded in the Torah. But, since they did not feel that they were "in exile," the Reformers also did away with the traditional second day of the festivals. Again, a bit of explanation is necessary.

When Jews first lived outside the Land of Israel, they had no way of knowing in advance exactly when the holidays began. The Hebrew calendar was not yet "fixed." Each month, when the new moon was seen, the authorities adjusted the Jewish lunar calendar to the sun cycle and figured out the proper time to celebrate the holidays. Then they sent signals and messengers to the outlying communities. Jews who lived outside Israel, knowing approximately when the holiday would come, began to double the first and last days of the holiday—the full festival days. That way, even if the news got to them late, they were certain to be observing the festival at the right time. As early as the middle of the fourth century C.E., astronomy had become exact enough that the Rabbis could create a permanent Jewish calendar. Jewish communities around the world continued to observe a second major day of festivals anyway, as a reminder that they were "in exile." The Reformers felt that the repetition of festival services was no longer needed or religiously desirable.

What Do We Still Mean by "The Messiah"?

The American Reformers (like their German predecessors) changed not only Jewish practices—the *way* of observing Judaism—but some old Jewish *beliefs* as well. One of these had to do with the Messiah. (See Chapter 19 for a specific discussion.) The Reform prayer book replaced all the traditional prayers asking for the coming of the Messiah with prayers for the coming of a Messianic Age, a time when all people would learn to live together in peace and harmony.

The Reformers found another traditional belief unacceptable. The Messiah's arrival was supposed to produce marvelous events, the most incredible being the resurrection of the dead. All the graves would open, people's souls would return to their purified bodies, and everyone would appear before God in Jerusalem for the Day of Judgment. Bodily resurrection seemed scientifically naive to the Reformers. Yet part of this religious belief appealed to them. They, too, had questions about human life that they were sure must have an answer: What puts the spark of life into matter? What makes humans the only animals with an extraordinary ability to think, sense right and wrong, and be aware of beauty? Why do human beings have "souls"? And what happens to the soul when a person dies? They could not altogether throw out the life-after-death concept. Instead, they used some old biblical and first-century Jewish ideas in a new way. They taught that when a person dies, only the body ceases. The "soul" lives on forever. This idea is called the immortality of the soul.

We have said that it was easy for the Reformers to make changes in America, but even here Reform did not have totally smooth sailing. The following true story should give you a clearer picture. At the end of the summer of 1850, when Isaac Mayer Wise was rabbi in a Reform congregation in Albany, New York, he took part in a panel discussion on religious beliefs. The spokesman for traditional Judaism asked Dr. Wise if he believed in the coming of the Messiah or in bodily resurrection. When Rabbi Wise said that he did not believe in either one, his answer shocked and horrified many members of his own congregation.

That Rosh Hashanah, when he entered the sanctuary to conduct services, he found someone else sitting in his seat on the *bimah*. He took another seat and said nothing. Everyone in the room was tense and silent. When it was time for the Torah service, Wise got up to open the ark. The president blocked his way. Wise tried to push past to get to the ark, but he never got there. He was punched in the face instead. The fighting spread to the whole congregation. The sheriff of Albany and his posse were called. They had trouble controlling the wildly angry, brawling crowd. All that over an *idea*! And in a congregation whose reforms already included a mixed choir, family pews, and an organ!

It is very important not to forget how emotional people get about the customs and ideas they have grown up with. Both the concept of making changes in religion and many of the Reform experiments are taken for granted today by most American Jews. Yet in the nineteenth century, and even among some people at the end of the twentieth century, any departure from the way their grandparents practiced Judaism seemed as bad to them as giving up Judaism altogether.

A New Prayer Book for New Beliefs

The Reformers had removed from their prayer books the parts of the service and the ideas that no longer made sense to them. They also added new prayers that expressed the way they felt. These prayers reflected their new sense of equality and the change it made in their outlook.

Reform Jews were among the pioneers who settled our country. In this picture, taken in 1911, Jewish proprietors pose with a group of Blackfoot Indians. One of the Indians, Two Guns White Calf, should look familiar to you. His profile appears on the Indian head nickel!

For them, equality was a deeply religious idea. They passionately believed that all people—whatever their religion—were essentially good and shared the same values. They did not think of themselves as a foreign element—Jews living, perhaps temporarily, in America—but as one group of Americans among all other Americans, following their own religious "persuasion."

The newly created Reform Jewish prayers reflected these ideals. The prayers spoke—in the usual masculine phrasing of that era—of the "brotherhood of man" and the universal "Fatherhood of God." This excerpt comes from the Union Prayer Book for Yom Kippur (1895):

> We, of the household of Israel, have been taught that the wrongs done to our fellowmen can be righted only if we think of all men as Thy children. When we are conscious of Thee as our common Father, we grow sensitive to the indignities and injustices visited upon our fellowmen. We realize that whatever does not serve to make our neighbor contented and trustful cannot receive Thy blessing and the sanction of Thy law.

The traditional prayer book said that Jews had been exiled from the ancient Land of Israel "for our sins." Reform Jews saw the scattering of the Jews as an ethical opportunity rather than as a punishment. They believed that the

DR. KAUFMANN KOHLER

Kaufmann Kohler, a German-born rabbi and a great scholar, became president of Hebrew Union College—the Reform rabbinical seminary—in 1903.

Jewish insistence on One God was the best basis for uniting all humanity, and the Jewish emphasis on law and study the best way of getting people to do good. Therefore, they felt that the Jewish people had a special mission in history. "The Mission of Israel," as they termed it, was to teach the world the universal values of truth and social justice.

Here are two early English translations of the second paragraph of the *Aleinu* (the Adoration)—one in the traditional prayer book and another in the Union Prayer Book. Note the subtle changes in the Reform reworking of the theme to express these ideas.

We therefore hope in thee, O Lord our God, that we may speedily behold the glory of thy might, when thou wilt remove the abominations from the earth, and the idols will be utterly cut off, when the world will be perfected under the kingdom of the Almighty, and all the children of flesh will call upon thy name, when thou wilt turn unto thyself all the wicked of the earth. Let all the inhabitants of the world perceive and know that unto thee every knee must bow, every tongue must swear. Before thee, O Lord our God, let them bow and fall; and unto thy glorious name let them give honor; let them all accept the yoke of thy kingdom, and do thou reign over them speedily, and for ever and ever. For the kingdom is thine, and all eternity thou wilt reign in glory; as it is written in thy Law, the Lord shall reign for ever and ever. And it is said, And the Lord shall be king over all the earth: in that day shall the Lord be One, and his name One.

May the time not be distant, O God, when Thy name shall be worshiped in all the earth, when unbelief shall disappear and error be no more. We fervently pray that the day may come when all men shall invoke Thy name, when corruption and evil shall give way to purity and goodness; when superstition shall no longer enslave the mind, nor idolatry blind the eye; when all inhabitants of the earth shall know that to Thee alone every knee must bend and every tongue give homage. O may all, created in Thine image, recognize that they are brethren, so that one in spirit and one in fellowship, they may be for ever united before Thee. Then shall Thy kingdom be established on earth and the word of Thine ancient seer be fulfilled: The Lord will reign for ever and ever.—On that day the Lord shall be One and His name shall be One.

Perhaps no prayer the Reform Jews created expressed their daring mixture of tradition and innovation as did this one, written by Kaufmann Kohler. It became part of the first Union Prayer Book (1895), and was probably the favorite prayer of American Reform Jews for most of the twentieth century:

Grant us peace, Thy most precious gift, O Thou eternal source of peace, and enable Israel to be a messenger of peace unto the peoples of the earth. Bless our country that it may ever be a stronghold of peace, and its advocate in the council of nations. May contentment reign within its borders, health and happiness within its homes. Strengthen the bonds of friendship and fellowship among all the inhabitants of our land. Plant virtue in every soul, and may the love of Thy name hallow every home and every heart. Praised be Thou, O Lord, Giver of peace.

Here is the traditional version, again in the translation of the late nineteenth century:

Grant peace, welfare, blessing, grace, lovingkindness and mercy unto us and unto all Israel, thy people. Bless us O our Father, even all of us together, with the light of thy countenance; for by the light of thy countenance thou hast given us, O Lord our God, the law of life, lovingkindness and righteousness, blessing, mercy, life and peace; and may it be good in thy sight to bless thy people Israel at all times and in every hour with thy peace. Blessed art thou, O Lord, who blessest thy people Israel with peace.

The Reform Jews felt at home in America. They prayed for their own community and for humanity as a whole. They were certain that a secure Jewish future lay in aiding general human progress, not in being isolated.

Events later in the twentieth century forced Reform Jews to take another look at this optimistic belief. But around the year 1900, when the primary concern of most Jews was adjusting to America and its freedom, and Western European Reform Jews were still the leaders of American Jewry, this enthusiasm for creative human potential seemed the proper response to the marvelous new opportunity American Jews were enjoying.

CHAPTER FOUR

Reform Jews and Other Jews in Our Day

Have you gone to services at a Conservative or Orthodox synagogue recently? Did the sanctuary look like yours? Was the prayer book unfamiliar? Was there a cantor? A choir? Organ music? If the occasion was a Bar or Bat Mitzvah, how did it compare to what you do at your temple?

It's easy to notice the ways that synagogues are different from one another. We are often surprised or even a little disturbed when something we expect doesn't happen or when something happens that we hadn't expected. But we tend to take for granted what we know. So you may not have realized that the synagogue you visited was quite similar to your own. For example, the congregation was most likely quiet, respectful, and well behaved. Probably, many prayers were read in English and there was a sermon, in English of course.

Nearly two hundred years ago, when Israel Jacobson and the other early Reformers introduced such practices they were considered shocking. Today, these and many other Reform innovations are accepted by almost all American Jews. Let's take a look at two new areas: Jewish art and Jewish music.

For a long time American Jews acted as if the only proper styles for ritual objects were the ones that had become popular in Europe when Jews

In designing ritual objects for home and synagogue, Jewish artists have always enriched their own creativity with ideas from the culture around them. (Top) This Hanukkiah of cast brass was made in seventeenth century Italy. (Bottom) This Hanukkiah was commissioned in 1950 by the Union of American Hebrew Congregations.

The simple lines of this silver *havdalah* set contrast sharply with the more ornate pieces of earlier periods.

were poor and oppressed. They became upset when modern artists designed Hanukkah menorahs and Torah covers. They didn't know what scholarship proves, that Jewish ritual objects have always been patterned after the artistic styles of whatever country Jews were living in. They didn't realize that by opposing contemporary Jewish art they were going against a major trend in Jewish history.

Think about the various Judaica objects you own or have seen. To take just one example: In your synagogue's Judaica shop alone there are probably lucite *hanukkiot*, or ceramic ones shaped like houses or like Maccabees, blown glass menorahs, or even stone and wooden ones that look like the Western Wall in Jerusalem. These lovely things help make our holidays especially beautiful—and give us pleasure throughout the year, whenever we look at them.

The same may be said of our Torah decorations. Silversmiths today favor simple, uncluttered lines. Their idea of a Torah crown or breastplate can bring us special joy when the Torah is taken from the ark.

Today, almost all American Jews appreciate modern styles of art for synagogue architecture, interior design, and ritual objects. It is hard to believe that Reform Jews once had a hard battle to get Judaism actively involved with contemporary culture.

31

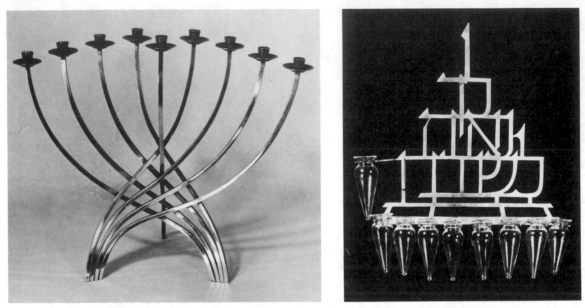

Ludwig Wolpert, one of the great modern Jewish craftsmen, created both of these Hanukkah menorahs. One is made of brass and the other of silver, lucite, and glass. Just as there are different styles of ritual objects, so too are there different choices for people within Judaism.

Music in the Synagogue

Perhaps the most important cultural victory was won in the area of Jewish music. When you visited another synagogue, were all the melodies familiar to you? Very likely some were identical to the ones in your synagogue, some were variations on the melodies you know and others were totally strange. This isn't surprising considering all the choices available. Jews have lived in many different countries, each with its own distinctive musical styles which were adapted for synagogue use. What is odd is how bitterly many Jews fought the idea of introducing *new* music to their services. They not only wanted the tunes they had grown up with, they wanted pretty much the same tunes week after week. For them, only these "traditional" melodies were considered appropriate at services.

It would be dreadful if every single response at services were sung with a new melody each week. All of us like to hear tunes we know well. Recognizing familiar melodies at another congregation makes you feel good and "at home." But liking what's new doesn't require changing all the time. "Modern" doesn't have to mean "disposable." It means allowing our composers to put Jewish prayers in new ways we may come to love. The Reform battle for modern Jewish music was another struggle to keep Judaism vital.

32

Jews Grow Closer Yet Stay Apart

Of course, Reform Judaism itself has changed over the years. Its experiments didn't all work out. Early Reform Jews were so interested in getting along with other Americans that they didn't give enough emphasis to strengthening their Jewish roots. Reform Jews in our time have moved to restore the balance with tradition, both because other Jews no longer fight so strongly against change and because the world has made Jewish survival as important a priority as adapting to democracy. Today most American Jewish congregations are very much alike. The old Reform Jewish notions about modern education, synagogue style, music, and art are generally accepted by American Jews. Mostly we disagree on *how* change should be made, *by whom* and *how quickly*. These issues create sharp divisions among our large Orthodox, Conservative, and Reform religious movements. We'll better understand what keeps them apart if we look closely at two troublesome (and related) problems: conversion, and religious equality in the State of Israel.

(Left) These silver *rimonim* were made in 18th century Germany. (Right) The second set, of cast tin, comes from North Africa.

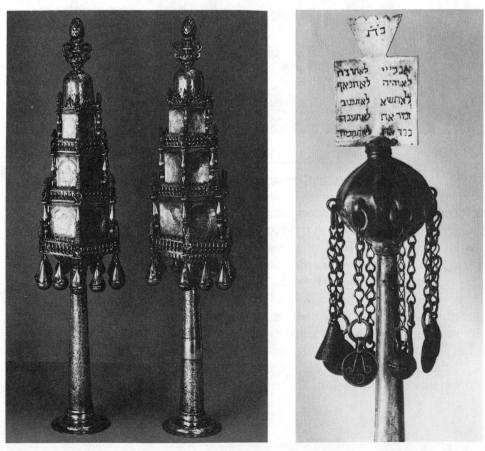

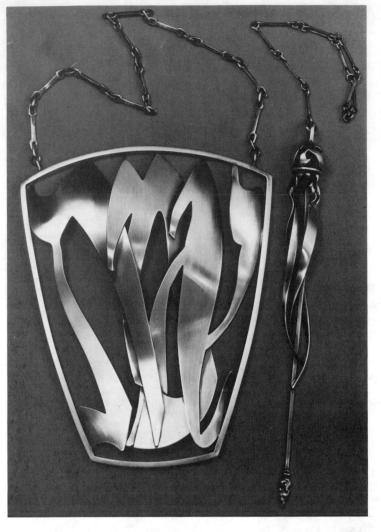

This very modern silver breastplate and pointer, the work of Maxwell Chayat, would not be appropriate with either set of *rimonim* on the previous page. Yet all are legitimate expressions of the creators' desire to beautify God's sanctuary.

When Does a Convert Really Become a Jew?

Reform Jewish practice clashes jarringly with the rulings of the Orthodox and Conservative movements in the area of conversion. The problem arises from the intimate contact Jews now regularly have with general society. A good many Jews today marry people raised in other religions. Many of these partners convert to Judaism. They first spend some time studying about Judaism. Then, if they follow the traditional conversion procedures they go through a ceremonial dip in a ritual bath (*mikveh*), and male converts become ritually circumcised. These procedures make the convert officially a Jew like every other Jew according to Jewish law.

The Reformers very early eliminated *mikveh* and circumcision as requirements for conversion. These rites seemed out of place in the modern world. They felt it would be much easier for people to convert to Judaism if such unusual requirements didn't exist. Of course they still insisted that would-be converts learn enough about Judaism to make intelligent decisions regarding being Jewish and living a Jewish life.

Orthodox and Conservative authorities say that converts who do not submit to all the traditional rituals have not become full Jews—and their children aren't "truly" Jewish either. Since Reform Jewish conversions are widely accepted in America, this often doesn't seem like an important difference between the groups. But occasionally problems do arise and, because they are so personal, they can be very upsetting. After all, Reform Jews do not live isolated from other Jewish groups. Let us explain.

Imagine for a moment that you are the child of a woman who was converted to Judaism by a Reform rabbi. Your mother did not go to the *mikveh* as part of her conversion. You, of course, have lived as a Jew since your birth. You have been attending religious school and look forward to being confirmed. You are a Jew—in your own mind and as far as the Reform movement is concerned. Yet, in the eyes of many Conservative and all Orthodox rabbis you are only part way toward being Jewish. They say *you* will need to be properly converted in order to be fully Jewish according to Jewish law. And if you move from your present community and become involved with another congregation this may cause you problems.

Suppose our imaginary "you" moves to another area with no Reform congregation. Pretend "you" are now a 12½-year-old boy. You have been studying for your Bar Mitzvah. You go with your parents to the local Orthodox rabbi to find a time for rescheduling your Bar Mitzvah. The rabbi asks some questions about your family and then says you can't become a Bar Mitzvah until you've first been converted, that you aren't really Jewish. (Or that he won't perform a wedding ceremony for "your" older sister because Jewish law doesn't consider her a Jew.) That would hurt a good deal.

These strict rabbis do not want to be unpleasant. There are just some things people feel that they can't compromise even for the sake of getting along together. For them Jewish law is too important to be changed easily, and in the area of family they are particularly careful to make changes very slowly.

Clearly the problem of acceptable conversions will continue to hurt individual Jews and seriously divide the Jewish community. Some Reform rabbis today feel that Reform Judaism has gone too far in removing the ancient rituals of conversion. They urge all the people they convert to go to the *mikveh*. They ask the men to undergo at least a symbolic *brit milah*. Other Reform rabbis feel very strongly that the traditional conversion rites no longer have a place in modern Judaism. They believe time and change will justify their opinion. The Reform view that a child born to a Jewish father and non-

Reform Judaism rejected the obligation of *mikveh* as a requirement for conversion, although many Reform rabbis encourage converts to go to the ritual bath as an act of solidarity with traditional Judaism. This eighteenth century engraving shows the *mikveh* in Amsterdam.

Jewish mother is "legally" Jewish—the concept known as "patrilineal" descent—makes agreement among the various movements less and less likely.

These differences of opinion are typical of the way things have been going ever since the rise of Reform.

Reform's Problems in the State of Israel

If "you" decide to move to the State of Israel the problem becomes far more serious. Israel is a democratic country, but it has no separation of "religion" and state. Orthodox Judaism is the official religion. While Christians, Moslems, and other religious groups are free to practice their religions as they wish, Orthodox Jews in the State of Israel control all Jewish religious matters. They set the rules and give out the government money for rabbis, synagogues, weddings, funerals, and other religious life-cycle events. More important, traditional Jewish law is the official law of the country for Jewish family matters. As a result, Reform or Conservative rabbis cannot legally marry people in Israel. If "your" sister wants to get married in Israel, she will first have to be converted by an Orthodox rabbi before he will perform the traditional Orthodox ceremony—the legally "official" one. Only then, if she wants to be married as a Reform Jew, can a Reform rabbi in Israel perform the "religious" ceremony.

There is a further complication if "you" want to become an Israeli citizen. Although non-Jews must formally immigrate, since 1950 any Jew (who is not a criminal) may become a citizen of Israel automatically. And for purposes of immigration, all people converted to Judaism outside Israel are officially accepted as Jews if they wish to settle in Israel. The Israeli government doesn't ask who performed the conversion. All people who say they are Jews are welcomed as full Israeli citizens under the Law of Return.

The Orthodox have been trying very hard to get the government's immigration law changed. They want the Israeli government to recognize only Orthodox conversions. As you can imagine, this has set off a rather bitter struggle in Israel, which sometimes affects relations among Jewish groups in America as well.

Some Orthodox extremists in the State of Israel are very intolerant of any liberalizing movements in Judaism. For some years now they have even published announcements in the Israeli newspapers "warning" people that it is a "greater sin" to attend a Conservative synagogue on the High Holy Days than to stay home from services!

A historic moment: Rabbi Alfred Gottschalk, President of HUC-JIR, blesses Mordecai Rotem, the first Israel-trained rabbinical student to be ordained in Israel.

How Much Shall We Modernize? How Fast Shall We Do It?

Changes *have* taken place in Orthodoxy over the centuries. But the Orthodox are not willing to alter anything until they are absolutely certain that what they will be doing is in accord with the two-thousand-year tradition of rabbinic law. Moreover, there is no "congress" or Sanhedrin to make final decisions about such matters. All over the world, Orthodox scholars scrupulously examine the Talmud and its commentaries to see what can and cannot be done. They are not eager to give their approval to anything that might "open the door" to heresy. These scholars feel that the Jewish community is threatened, and that they must protect the continuity of Judaism through strict observance.

Conservative Jews also worry about making hasty decisions to alter Jewish practices, but they are more willing to consider the possibility of change. The Conservative rabbis have established a Law Commission to determine what changes are appropriate to our social situation. It has permitted a large number of changes, particularly in recent years, like permitting women to be called up to the Torah. These changes have stirred up controversy within the Conservative movement. Some Conservative Jews argue that the rate of change is too fast; others say it is too slow.

Reform Jews believe that if something is good and proper to do, like making women fully equal to men in Judaism, it should become effective as soon as people see the need. According to Reform, every Jew should have the right to decide how to live as an individual and as a Jew. Of course, choices involving God, the Torah, and ethics are very serious matters, and people who intend to take their responsibility seriously need to know a lot about Judaism and what Jews believe.

The overwhelming majority of American Jews takes a very practical approach to their Jewish duties. They may listen respectfully to what their rabbis tell them about scholarly decisions, but they usually make up their own minds about the kind of Jewish life they will lead. In effect, and regardless of what they call themselves, they follow the Reform Jewish way of personal responsibility—although, unfortunately, most of them are not as thoughtful and sincere about building their Judaism as Reform teachers would like them to be.

CHAPTER FIVE

What All Jews Share

This book explains Reform Judaism. To make it stand out, we often stress the differences between Reform Jews and other Jews. Because we make these comparisons, most of the things that Reform Jews *share* with other Jews will not be mentioned. They are not what make Reform Jews special.

That may be confusing. You may conclude that the most important thing about Reform Jews is how different they are from other Jews. If so, we will have given you the wrong impression. The most important thing about Reform Jews and other Jews is that, *all things considered*, they are very much more like one another than different from each other.

Before going any further into this book, then, let's stop and look at some examples of what Reform shares with the rest of Judaism.

We Are One Religion — with Different Aspects

There are many different ways to be Jewish or live a Jewish life. Most Jews are born into the Jewish community. The traditional definition of a "born Jew" is the child of a Jewish mother. Some people choose to become Jewish and convert to Judaism. Once a person is part of the Jewish religion further choices are possible. Some Jews are Orthodox and follow traditional Jewish law faithfully. But not all Orthodox Jews are alike. There are Orthodox Jews who support the State of Israel and Orthodox Jews who oppose it. There are Hasidic and non-Hasidic Orthodox Jews. There are some Orthodox Jews who accept modern ways—like going to a university—and others who try to avoid them.

Then there are Conservative Jews, who differ from the Orthodox about the speed and manner in which we should modernize Judaism. And there is an offshoot of the Conservative movement called Reconstructionism. Some Reform Jews, the most flexible group, are quite traditional in their practices. Other Reform Jews are far less so. Obviously, there is a whole range of ways of thinking about Judaism and of acting on Jewish beliefs.

There are also differences of style between Ashkenazi Jews and Sephardi Jews. Ashkenazim (the word originally meant "Germans") are Jews from northern Europe. Sephardim (originally "Spaniards") come from Spain, Italy, and other Mediterranean countries. Most American Jews have Ashkenazi roots, but the number of Sephardim has increased in recent years.

Not too long ago, German-American Ashkenazim and East European Ashkenazim in America felt that their way of life had little in common with one another. They even fought against "intermarriages" between their children. A similar hostility exists among Sephardi Jews in Europe today. Sephardim born in France and Sephardim who have emigrated from North Africa reside in the same neighborhoods. Yet for all practical purposes, they live in quite different religious and cultural worlds.

Despite these differences—and there are many others—all of these people are Jews. So they share certain beliefs, ideas, and concerns.

Tradition, Traditions

The opening song of *Fiddler on the Roof* is called "Tradition." It captures in a humorous way the most important thing all Jews share. When the poor, suffering Jews of Anatevka ask, "Why do we do the things we do?" they really know the answer. They say, "It is our way. It is 'tradition'."

It's useful to divide Jewish tradition into two parts. The first is really traditions—all those customs and habits that seem natural to us because we've "always" done them in a particular way. Americans eat hot dogs and hamburgers at cookouts. People stand during the seventh inning of a baseball game because people "always" do that. You can probably think of some traditions in your own family. And the same is true of our religious "family," the Jews.

There are many different styles of Jewish observance. Left: Hasidic children playing together on the street. Below: Despite differences in observance, most Jews are united by some basic beliefs, as well as concern for the future and security of their people. Bottom: Sephardic Jews in a 1954 ceremony marking the three hundredth anniversary of the Spanish and Portuguese Synagogue of New York.

The other meaning of tradition is more formal and official. When we speak of the Jewish tradition we often think of its most important books and documents, chiefly the Bible and the Talmud. But the tradition isn't limited to them. The tradition includes the whole system of beliefs and practices that has been worked out through the centuries since the Torah was written down.

While specific Jewish traditions vary from location to location and from group to group—for instance, Sephardi Jews don't think chopped liver or gefilte fish are "traditional" Jewish foods—all Jews share the same Jewish tradition. For guidance they look to the Bible, the Talmud, the Midrash, and all the other books written over the centuries by the Rabbis. All have synagogues that focus on a Torah scroll whose contents are identical to that of every other Torah scroll in the world. And all agree that these first five books of the Bible are uniquely holy.

Through the Year and Through Life

All Jews follow the same religious calendar. They celebrate the same holidays and observe their rituals on the same days everywhere in the world. They even have the same conception of a "day." For every Jew, Shabbat begins at sundown on Friday evening and ends on Saturday night. True, Israeli and Reform Jews observe a holiday for one day while other Jews observe it for two.

Many American *bnai mitzvah* have "twinned" with the children of refusenik families in the Soviet Union who are not free to study Hebrew and Jewish subjects.

And the foods, games, and songs that different Jews use in their celebrations vary from place to place and group to group. But if you are in Buenos Aires or in Stockholm next year for Yom Kippur, you'll know exactly when to go looking for the local service—and much of what is read and chanted will be familiar to you.

Similarly, in the cycle from birth through death all Jews follow the same pattern. We all agree that certain life events are special—birth, marriage, and death are the chief examples—and all Jews mark them with similar religious rites. Since Bar Mitzvah is certainly familiar to you, let's study it for a moment.

Bar Mitzvah normally takes place as close as possible to the thirteenth birthday, on a day when the Torah is read. The Bar Mitzvah ceremony involves having an *aliyah*, saying the blessings and reading from the Torah scroll. If it takes place on Shabbat, the Bar Mitzvah will chant the *haftarah* (the prophetic portion of the day) and its blessings. The Bar Mitzvah's family and friends will be at the service to share in the pleasure and honor. They will all join afterward in some sort of party where there will be lots of eating and drinking and rejoicing. True, some who are called to the Torah as a Bar Mitzvah will chant their portions while others will read them. Some will lead parts or all of the service, some will deliver a speech and many others will do none of these things. Some services will be long and some short. Some synagogues have Bat Mitzvah. Jews do differ. But the main thing is that for all of them Bar Mitzvah is a "coming of age." And they all celebrate it with the same basic ceremonies and in pretty much the same spirit.

All Jews are part of the same people. As one people, we have a common language. The Bible and most of the Jewish traditional literature are written in Hebrew. At services, our prayers are either in Hebrew or are English versions of the Hebrew prayers.

If you have ever traveled, you may have visited a country where the people spoke a language you couldn't understand. But if you met any Jews, you could say "shalom" and there would be an instant bond between you. Although most Jews worldwide only use Hebrew for prayer or study, in the State of Israel it is the everyday language.

We Share Some Common Historical Memories

Two things that happened in the twentieth century continue to influence the lives of caring Jews. The terrible one, the Holocaust, unites all Jews in remembering the horrifying Jewish loss and suffering. And those who "remember" now include many who have only heard about it long after it happened or have seen pictures of what was done.

Our people stands united in its determination that nothing like the Holocaust will ever happen again. We must work together to build the Jewish future.

David Ben-Gurion, the first Prime Minister of Israel.

The State of Israel, on the other hand, is the pride and joy of Jews everywhere. Israel's work in admitting refugees, making the country green, and caring for all its citizens is a source of happiness to all Jews. Israel's military victories have given new courage to our people, particularly those suffering oppression in places like the former Soviet Union. Wherever in the world Jews live, Israel is somehow part of them and they are connected to Israel. Jews therefore work together for Israel's security and to help assure its future. They want the best for Israel, and they want Israel to set the best possible example for everyone else.

Jews Reach Out to Help One Another

A Jewish teaching says, "Everyone of the Jewish people is responsible for everyone else." And that means especially in bad times. Jewish people worried for many years about the distressing situation for the millions of their brethren who lived in the Soviet Union. The Soviet government not only made it hard for them to live openly as Jews, but made it hard for them to leave. Worse, it made their lives miserable once they said they wanted to go. World Jewry worked hard to open up Soviet emigration and will continue to work on behalf of these Jews and other Jews who may be in trouble.

In America, Jews of all backgrounds and religious groups work together very closely. Reform Jews, Orthodox Jews, Conservative Jews, Reconstructionists and Jews who do not belong to congregations join to run their UJA/Federation campaigns to collect funds for general humanitarian causes and to see to it that needy Jews can find help. Other community organizations like Hadassah, ORT, the National Council for Jewish Women, the American Jewish Congress, American Jewish Committee, and B'nai B'rith are also made up of Jews from different backgrounds, with different religious outlooks. They try to help all Jews live better Jewish lives and they fight to eliminate prejudice and discrimination from American life.

And, though it sounds odd to say so, all Jews have the same future in common. When one group of Jews is suffering, the rest are soon likely to suffer too; and when one group of Jews triumphs, the remainder share in the glory.

The State of Israel is the Jewish homeland, offering a place of refuge for Jews throughout the world. The documents pictured here show that this couple, who left the Soviet Union, made their way to Israel via Austria.

All Jews Have the Same God

For all religious Jews, belief in God is at the center of being Jewish. They agree that God should be served through prayer, education, good deeds, *tzedakah*, rituals, and making the world a better place to live. All faithful Jews believe that there is only one God in the universe and that the Jewish people taught the world about that one God. This belief has distinguished Jews over the generations. That's what the *shema* is all about.

All Jews believe that everyone can pray to God at any time. Jews pray together as a community in the synagogue because all Jews believe that they share their religion as members of the Jewish people and not just as private individuals. But Jews also believe that God is available whenever a person turns to God with any words, in any language, or with song or in silence.

Since the days of the prophets, Jews have said that the best way of serving God is through the right kind of living and acting. Particularly in modern times, as people have had more freedom to do good or evil, Jews have been concerned about treating everyone fairly and helping those who could not help themselves. For all Jews, being an ethical human being is an important part of serving God and being a good Jew.

We Are One Family — But We Do Not Have Just One Way

The Bible and the prayer book call the Jewish people the "children of Israel." In one sense, they mean it literally. Israel is the name Jacob got after wrestling with the angel, according to the Book of Genesis. The "children of Israel" means Jacob's family by birth or by choice: *all* Jews. Customs, ideas, and attitudes vary from one group to another. Still, all Jews know they belong to "one family." And that brings us back to comparing Reform Jews with other Jews. As in your own family, people develop individual styles and want to do things their own way. That sometimes causes disagreement. But it doesn't take away their membership in the family, or your basic concern for their well-being or theirs for you.

What we have been saying in this chapter is that Reform Jews are full members of the Jewish family. And not all Jews like the Reform way of being Jewish.

Some Jews feel that those who do not follow all of the traditions they themselves follow are not good Jews. They insist that their way is the only right Jewish way. They think it was wrong of Reform Judaism to introduce changes into the religion and that Reform Jewish freedom is a mistake. Yet, with all that, they do not say that Reform Jews aren't Jewish. They do not question the fact that Reform Jews are part of the Jewish family. That's why they are so unhappy about Reform. They want Reform Jews to be *their* kind of Jews.

What do you do when others criticize you? If they are right, you try not to show you're upset over what they have said, and you make an effort to learn from the experience. But if you honestly feel they are wrong, you must stand up for what you believe is right—even if they don't like it.

The critics of Reform Judaism are much less harsh today than they were in the years when Israel Jacobson was creating a modern style for Jewish services at his school. Most Jews not only feel much closer to what Reform Jews have stood for, they have quietly adopted many Reform ideas. In that way, too, the Jews are a family. Although Jews may sometimes quarrel fiercely with one another, an outsider can see that for all the squabbling Jews resemble each other very much.

So don't be confused. Very much more ties Reform Jews to all other Jews than separates us from them. But what *separates* us is what makes us a unique group *within* Judaism. We keep emphasizing what makes Reform Jews different from other Jews because we take for granted what unites us and makes us one people. We hope you will keep that in mind as you read this book.

ISAAC M. WISE
1819-1900

PART TWO

Who Tells Reform Jews What to Do and Believe?

Reform Jews can choose for themselves not only what they believe but also how they will act as Jews. This freedom of choice is most unusual in religion, because almost all of the world's faiths emphasize discipline and obedience.

Why should Reform Judaism want to stress the freedom to think for oneself? Don't many people abuse their freedom, using it to do stupid and even dangerous things? How does that fit with caring about other people's rights? With continuing Judaism's long history? With being loyal to God? With sharing responsibility for Jews everywhere in the world, and keeping alive the old Jewish dream of a messianic age? How can Reform Jews stay together as a united group if they put such stress on personal choice?

These are some of the questions we hope to answer in the chapters ahead.

CHAPTER SIX

The Reform Jewish Emphasis on Personal Freedom

When you were little, you weren't permitted to cross the street by yourself. When you got older, the situation changed. Your mother and father may have worried when you started going to school alone but they knew you had to do it. If they didn't give you the freedom to cross the street when you thought it was safe, you'd never grow up. As you got older, you got wiser, so the rules about what you could do had to change.

And because you are even more thoughtful now, you deserve a lot of freedom. The amount of freedom you should have is an issue that can cause many arguments. Parents often do not seem to see how much their children have grown. They get used to the idea of their little ones being young and helpless, needing them for everything. They want to be needed and they like being helpful, so they don't realize that after a while they are no longer being helpful but overprotective. It hurts them to hear "I can do it myself," even though they know that the most important part of growing up is learning to make responsible independent decisions.

Parents also know that there are good and bad ways of using freedom. If you are supposed to buy lunch in school and spend the money on cola and potato chips instead, you are using your independence foolishly. But many people do far worse things than that. They so misuse their freedom that they hurt themselves and others, sometimes quite badly.

Soon you will be old enough to get a driver's license. Think of getting the car key, opening the door, slipping into the driver's seat, starting the engine, and going wherever you want to go. What freedom that will mean! What power! But how will you use it? Will you be careful? Or will you let people dare you into racing or speeding or playing "chicken"? Will you and your friends become another sickening statistic in the record that shows year after year that young people get into more fatal accidents than any other group of drivers?

Growing up to be sensible isn't easy. Some adults seem never to have learned it. When they are under pressure, they behave like infants. They throw tantrums or sulk or won't cooperate. Then we say, "They're behaving like babies." A major part of growing up is learning to control childish feelings in order to make proper decisions. It requires serious judgment to decide when doing what everyone else does is right and when it is a mistake; or when it's time to try something new and when it is wiser to wait awhile. Each of us has to judge by ourself and for ourself. Otherwise we are not free—and we are not responsible.

Learning how best to use our freedom is the hardest and most important part of growing up. It can't be learned in a single lesson or at a particular age. We have to keep learning new ways of being responsible all our lives, for we keep changing as we grow older.

Before we apply these ideas about being grown-up to Reform Judaism, let's take a look at how freedom came into our social institutions.

Why Were People Less Free Before?

The United States was brought into existence by people who believed that personal freedom is a natural human right. Although we can't imagine ourselves living without freedom it was a very new idea then. In fact, it is still a controversial idea today. Personal liberty has been the exception, not the rule, throughout human history.

Why is that? How can anyone be against liberty?

Many people consider freedom dangerous because it can lead to change. The privileged leaders who have all the power certainly don't want anything taken away from them. Do bullies ever want to share? That is why so much of the world has been ruled by kings or dictators.

Sometimes changes that promise good things end up taking away freedom. What the Nazis did to Germany is one example. What the Communists did in the former Soviet Union is another. Many people who would enjoy true

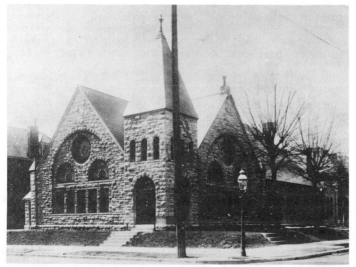

The wide variations in synagogue architecture show the way secular society influences Jewish cultural styles. Counterclockwise from above: Temple Beth Tefilloh, Brunswick, Ga.; Isaiah Temple, Chicago; Temple Sholom, Chicago; United Hebrew Congregation, St. Louis.

freedom are therefore afraid of great changes, like revolutions, because they know there is always the risk that they'll end up worse off than before.

Some fear the changes that come from new ideas. These changes challenge what people "always" believed. Imagine the shock of the first people who realized that the sun doesn't go around the earth. Their whole sense of truth and certainty fell apart. "Modern times" began when people started realizing that the past didn't have all the truth. Scientists made remarkable discoveries that radically changed peoples' ideas about nature. Pioneers in France and America experimented with equality and showed that "we, the people" could establish a better kind of government than one given by the "divine right" of kings.

The Democratic Spirit Gives Rise to Reform Judaism

As the idea of democracy spread from France to the rest of Western Europe in the late 1700s and the early 1800s, some religious teachers saw a surprising connection between democracy and religion. They suggested that individuals ought to have greater religious freedom just as they now had greater political freedom. Now, they said, people should have the right not only to decide who would govern them politically but what beliefs would rule their lives.

In this way, the idea of democracy created the "liberal" movements in European religion.

Reform pioneered liberal Judaism. It brought democracy into the Jewish religion in ways unlike anything ever tried before. For example, a central teaching of Reform Judaism is that all Jews have the right to make up their own minds about how to be Jewish. Orthodox Jews think of the Jewish tradition as something Jews *must* observe because God commanded it. They believe that the Torah is far more reliable than any individual's mind or conscience. Therefore, even if they personally disagree with a traditional rule, like the teachings of the Rabbis on women's rights, they stifle their objections and do what the Sages say the Torah teaches.

Reform Jews see Jewish tradition as one of the best guides they have to help them use their minds wisely. Reform Judaism does not teach that the Torah contains God's own words. Instead, Reform Jews think that Torah developed as our wisest and most sensitive ancestors understood in their consciences what God "wanted" them to do. Over the centuries, many such geniuses taught our people how to be good Jews. And today, when wise Jews sense that God wants them to do something different from what Jews did in ancient or medieval (pre-modern) times, they must, as good Jews, follow the new path that they know is right. That is a key part of Reform Judaism's devotion to freedom.

What happens when Reform Jews use this freedom to decide things for themselves? Sometimes an old law or custom is abolished—like separating men and women at services. Sometimes thinking about a tradition may get Reform Jews to add to their observance—like having a lot of Hebrew in services. In any case, Reform Jewish teachers encourage everyone to use their consciences and their knowledge of Judaism to help them make up their own minds. This means that not every Reform Jew has to do the same thing as every other Reform Jew—but all must think for themselves as seriously and wisely as possible.

One hotly argued old case where Reform Jews insisted on their freedom deals with riding on Shabbat. The Rabbis of the Talmud had ruled that Jews must not ride anytime during Shabbat. What was their reason?

Until the invention of cars, a family that wanted to go anywhere far away had to first harness a horse to their wagon or carriage. When they arrived they had to unharness, feed the horse, give it water, perhaps brush it down. And they had to go through the same routine when they went home again. The

This picture of the Albany Hebrew Congregation synagogue in Albany, Georgia, was taken in the early days of the automobile. Whatever their style, all synagogues share certain features. Can you name some of them?

decision forbidding riding seems to have had this kind of hard work in mind. Besides, long ago Jews used to live very near each other and their synagogue, so they could walk practically everywhere they might have wanted to go during Shabbat.

Today, our lives are built around cars. Many people live quite far from their synagogue. What do you think is more in the spirit of a modern Shabbat? To stay at home, away from the synagogue, because Jewish tradition prohibits driving on Shabbat? Or to get into the car and go to services? What about also using the car for a special trip to visit family or friends or a museum?

But such freedom raises new questions and causes new problems. Once it is okay to drive on Shabbat, will Shabbat simply become Saturday, a day like every other day? Will Jews go rushing around from place to place, exhausting themselves in the process, annoyed by other drivers and forgetting that Shabbat is a day of rest and not the right time to run errands and catch up on chores?

Often we can see new reasons for old practices. The Torah law about not riding seems to have guaranteed that the family would be together at least once a week. Wouldn't it be nice for the entire family to spend some time together when there is no school and parents aren't working? Is having that bit of relaxed family time each week sufficient reason not to use the car on Shabbat? Or would using the car to do some things together make it a better Shabbat? Reform Jews don't have just one answer to such questions. Reform Jews are each expected to make such decisions for their own lives. Reform Judaism says, "Be responsible for yourself." Its democracy goes that far.

The Advantages and the Problems of Jewish Freedom

The great freedom Reform Judaism gives to each person can cause problems like those in the story of the Tower of Babel. So long as everyone spoke the same language they worked together toward a common goal—however selfish and dangerous that goal may have been. When they no longer understood each other, the whole project collapsed. That can happen to any democracy if people care only about what is good for them personally and ignore their society. That is certainly true about Judaism, for we are a small people and need a lot of cooperation if we are to survive.

Even worse, many people make unwise use of their right to think for themselves. They follow their moods instead of their conscience and wind up causing harm and getting hurt. Maybe that's why there are so few democracies in the world today. People abuse the privilege of freedom. They aren't grown-up enough to take it as seriously as it must be taken.

We must be honest: Most Jews today misuse their freedom to be Jewish. Many do nothing at all about their Jewish duties. Others simply do whatever is easiest for them or makes them feel good. Few people seriously ask what it means for them to be good Jews.

Then why does Reform Judaism emphasize Jewish freedom when so many people misuse it? Why let people make their own choices if they keep acting so unwisely?

Reform Judaism, like democracy, truly believes in people—at least in people *as they ought to be and can become*. If we turn our backs on freedom, people will never have the chance to become the kind of full human beings God uniquely created us to be. Therefore, Reform Judaism continues trying to help modern Jews accept religious freedom and learn to use it responsibly, despite people's foolishness, stupidity, and pettiness. The leaders and institutions of Reform Judaism may not always have given the kind of guidance they should have given, and Reform Jews have regularly resisted taking Jewish duty seriously—even though they are free to decide for themselves as individuals just what their "Jewish duty" should mean. But that doesn't make the goal less important. A modern democratic Judaism continues to be an ideal well worth working for.

CHAPTER SEVEN

Changing Times and the Changes in Reform Judaism

T he early American Reformers didn't just enter the general society, they *believed in it* and its new freedom. Everywhere they looked they saw continual progress. Science was discovering new truths. Education was ending ignorance. And industry was producing a flood of goods that led to a higher standard of living. For the Jews, too, despite some setbacks, everything seemed to be getting better. It made no sense to them to continue a ghetto-style Jewish life. So the pioneers of Reform eagerly gave up whatever Jewish practices seemed to stand in the way of full participation in American life.

When other Jews criticized the Reformers, they answered with one of their new Jewish creations: modern scholarship. Careful study of the Jewish past, they insisted, showed that Jews had always changed their religious observance in response to major social change. Their most powerful example was the Temple.

The Traumatic Change of 70 C.E.

When the Temple was destroyed by the Romans, Jews could no longer worship as the Torah instructed. How, then, could they properly serve God?

To those of us living now, the answer seems obvious—a change was necessary and it was made. The Rabbis shifted the emphasis in Judaism from the grandeur of the Temple pageant to the Jewish home and the everyday life of ordinary Jews. They also created the synagogue, where worship could be led by any Jew who knew how. This "reform" substituted everyone's prayer, study and observance for the Temple sacrifices in which only the priests were personally involved. Therefore, it made Judaism more meaningful to most Jews. It took time for them to become comfortable with it, but they did. By not stubbornly holding on to their old way as the only way of being good Jews, they saved Judaism and allowed the Jewish people to survive.

Modern Changes

The Reformers believed that the Emancipation had radically changed the world Jews lived in. They felt, once again, that Judaism would have to change in order to remain vital. Some of their changes sound unimportant to us, like giving up separate clothing styles or ways of cutting one's hair or beard. Yet these and many other "little" changes shocked a lot of people greatly. Far more significant was the freedom Reform gave people with regard to the laws which set the Jews apart, like keeping kosher and scrupulously observing the Shabbat restrictions. From it, too, came the creativity which enabled them to Americanize the synagogue.

Modernizing Jews also believed that being a good Jew ought first of all to mean being an ethical person. Now that Jews were part of society, acting decently toward non-Jews became a major new religious duty. The Reformers unhesitatingly taught that "love your neighbor as yourself" meant caring for all people, not just for Jews. In a democracy, working for everyone's good was not a matter of choice; it had to be a major Jewish obligation.

Some radical Jews went even farther. They said that the ethical ideals of America were the same as the values taught by Judaism, so why worry about Judaism at all? For them, being a good American was the best way of being a good Jew. They made America—not Judaism—their religion. They exercised their freedom to give up their duties and responsibilities as Jews. They represent the extreme of the Reform use of freedom—but we can learn from them what happens when freedom is only negative ("freedom not-to-do"), and not also positive ("freedom to do").

Increasingly, most modern Jews were dismayed by people who used their freedom to run away from Judaism. They felt that another sort of change was necessary. They began a new phase of Reform Judaism, one in which Reform Jews are encouraged to use their freedom to choose what they will *do* as Jews.

When the Second Temple was destroyed and its menorah carried off (as shown here on the Arch of Titus in Rome) many Jews feared that the end of their world had come. But Judaism survived as our people learned how to adapt to changing conditions. Reform Judaism has retained that ancient Jewish ability.

Shattered Illusions: The Holocaust

Several historical events helped bring about this new attitude. The most devastating was the Holocaust. From 1939 to 1945, European Jewry was destroyed by the Nazis. Six million Jews were murdered, among them almost one and half million children. They were killed simply because they were Jewish and, according to the insane Nazi philosophy, Jews didn't deserve to live.

The Holocaust altered Jewish ideas about democracy in two critical ways. The first was that modern Jews must devote a good part of their energy not merely to the general society in which they live, but also to keeping the Jewish people alive. We Jews are a tiny and often quite vulnerable people. If Jews do not watch out for one another and help one another, we cannot expect

Through this game—*JUDEN RAUS!* or "Jews, get out"—young German children were taught to hate Jews.

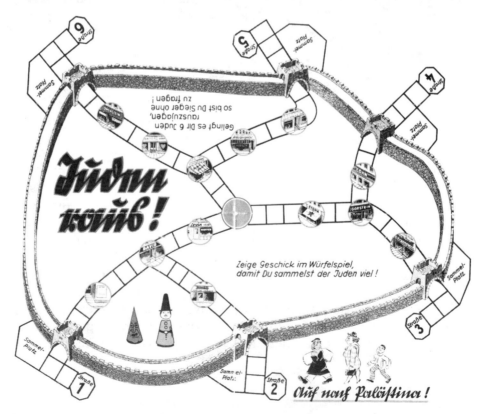

anyone else to do so. Despite centuries of democracy, anti-Semitism remains alive and dangerous—even in democratic countries. Anti-Semitism does not distinguish between "good" and "bad" citizens among the Jews. Its poison works indiscriminately against all Jews. So every Jew must give a good part of his or her energy to strengthening the Jewish people and fighting off our enemies.

The second lesson was that the practice of democracy, despite all its great virtues, was no substitute for practicing one's religion. Many Nazis were well-educated people who knew music and literature. They were kind parents, caring friends. Yet they treated Jews like rats or other vermin, not human beings. Liberal Jews had thought that educated people everywhere would not be swayed by crude propaganda or mass-hysteria, that they were incapable of committing barbaric acts. They learned they had been too optimistic. The basic goodness of people is balanced by a deep, dark potential for doing evil. To rid the world of inhumanity will take more than getting a good education or living in a democracy. It will take, at the least, deep faith and steady devotion—and God's help.

Concern for Our Group as Well as for Every Group

The world's indifference to the Holocaust further shattered Reform Jews' old religious trust in humanity. Millions of innocent people were being killed, yet the world stayed silent. American officials barred the admission of thousands of people desperately trying to flee Europe. Even American Jewish leaders, when they learned about the Nazi death camps, kept silent because they trusted the goodwill of the American government. Almost no one cried out at the destruction of much of European Jewry.

Worse, when American Jewish groups asked the Allied governments to bomb the rail lines to the death camps, they were told that the men and materiel could not be spared. Years later, Jews learned of repeated U.S. bombing missions over German factory installations only a few miles from Auschwitz. Why then did the American government lie? One reason may be anti-Semitism. When otherwise quite decent people are in positions of authority, they can endanger the rights of groups they look down on, perhaps unconsciously. That happened to us during World War II; it has happened to us and many other minority groups in the years since then. None of us should automatically put the general society before our own welfare. We also have to be active in our own defense—and in protecting the rights of all other minority groups as well. Giving Judaism up for democracy hurts both. Religion as well as politics must have an important place in our lives.

Other sad developments in recent years showed Reform Jews that they ought to be as concerned with their Judaism as with the modern world. One aspect of this has been the continual revelation that trusted officials have deceived us. A similar kind of disappointment has come with the growth of knowledge. Scientific discoveries, which once seemed to bring new wonders to us endlessly, have also created grave new dangers. Look at nuclear power, for instance. Nuclear medicine has brought the hope of cures for diseases that not long ago were fatal. But nuclear bombs can destroy the world. And what is true of nuclear science is true of psychology, bioengineering, and almost any other field you can think of. We need Judaism's age-old religious wisdom to help us face the modern world and to guide us in putting our new knowledge to good uses.

Judaism with Freedom — and Hope

Some people who agree with the need for religion in our lives cannot face being free to think for themselves. They want religious answers but they don't want to have to make their own decisions—and so many join a cult. People who belong to cults are "sure" that the cult is right and its teacher is infallible. Surrounded by fellow believers they don't have to worry about whether or not they are making correct choices. They willingly give up their adult responsibility in exchange for their certainty.

Reform Judaism stands for exactly the opposite way of facing life. It teaches that individuals have a unique talent for thinking and deciding for themselves and ought to use it—even in religion. Reform is against cults not only because Judaism disagrees with most cult ideas about God, but also be-

The State of Israel continues to give Jews pride and joy in being Jewish. At this celebration marking Israeli independence, a girl's shirt reads "Shalom!"—a greeting and a fervent wish for peace.

The opening of the Maccabiah Games in Israel, which attracts athletes from around the world.

cause cults destroy our most important freedom, the freedom to use our minds and consciences to rule our lives.

Happily, contemporary Reform Jews have positive reasons for putting more emphasis on their Judaism. One is the growth and success of the State of Israel.

Earlier in this century, most Jews could not imagine what extraordinary things their people would accomplish working together in their own country. The Israeli accomplishments in farming, in science, in culture—in building a society which cares for its citizens—have been phenomenal compared to other young countries. And when one remembers that a large number of its citizens are survivors of the Holocaust or refugees from Arab countries, the Israeli achievement is breathtaking. The way the Israelis have faced unceasing political and military pressure, including terrorism, without giving up their vigorous democracy is without parallel in the modern world. For all these reasons, and many more, as American Jews were becoming more concerned with Judaism, the State of Israel gave them new pride and joy in being Jewish.

A banner quotes the motto of the STAR WARS movies at the annual Israel Day parade in New York City.

A second thing has made it easy for liberal Jews to give greater attention to Judaism: American Jews have created their own style of being Jewish—and it is very attractive. No other Jewry has had our sort of summer camps for children and conclaves for youth, our Friday evening services followed by cake and coffee and conversation, our intensive fund-raising campaigns, our mixture of university education and Jewish communal involvement—to name only a few of the things that excite Jewish visitors to America. This American Jewish style is a subtle blend of American push and practicality with Jewish idealism and folk loyalty.

Put simply, American Jews now can feel very much at ease being both Americans and Jews. Jewish teen-agers who wear six-pointed stars, or *chais*, or *mezuzot* are all announcing publicly that they are proud to be Jewish. So are the people who march in Israel Day parades and take part in public Jewish events, and those who participate in interfaith *seders* with churches in their communites. They know, in a new and positive way, that it's good to be a Jew. The fact that many other groups in America feel the same way about their unique traditions has helped to make it easier for Jews to be proud of their Judaism and take it more seriously.

Choosing in New Ways

So with the general society far from a messianic age, with the Jewish people in need and deserving of major Jewish attention, most Reform Jews have moved into a new phase of using their freedom. It has now become freedom to live a more fully Jewish life. A new time has produced a new response.

In the first phase, Reform Jews pioneered in fitting Judaism into American life. They emphasized their separateness from traditional Jewish patterns. In recent years, Reform Jews have begun to use their freedom to strengthen Jewish life in America and, of course, in the State of Israel. This has led Reform Jews to be more interested in being like all other Jews and has affected their religious practice, particularly in their congregations. In most services there is more Hebrew than there used to be. In some, many men now wear a *kippah* when praying. Bar and Bat Mitzvah have become the rule instead of the exception. The latest Reform prayer book, *Gates of Prayer*, was made available with pages opening from right to left, in the Hebrew direction. And in more and more Reform Jewish homes, Shabbat and festivals are marked with special ceremony.

We are not suggesting that all Reform Jews have now begun to take their Jewish obligations seriously. Unfortunately, too many still think Reform Judaism teaches only the freedom to do little or nothing. But what has excited us and many observers of the American scene is the new positive attitude that one finds in Reform Judaism today, with people using their freedom to be loyal, observing Jews. We do not know how long this phase of Reform's history will last or what will, in time, succeed it. But if the early Reformers had not had the courage to break with their ghetto past, we would not have the joy of seeing Reform Jews today use their freedom to adopt old Jewish ways to build a new way of life.

CHAPTER EIGHT

The Limits of Reform Jewish Freedom

Did you ever drive a bumper car at an amusement park? Steering straight at other cars and making crazy turns can be lots of fun. You don't have to be cautious about how you drive because the cars are made to let you bump safely. But sometimes you find that you can't control the car. No matter which way you turn the steering wheel, the car continues on its own course. That's scary for a moment, even though you know that really you are safe.

Driving a real car is serious business because you aren't always safe. If a car gets out of control, even briefly, people can get very badly hurt. Making an automobile move is easy. But driving responsibly isn't child's play.

That's why people must earn the right to drive. A driver's license is more than simple permission to operate a car. It means the driver knows the rules of the road and agrees to obey them—or suffer heavy penalties. A driver who breaks the rules by speeding or driving recklessly can be fined or lose his or her license or even be jailed. The punishment is designed to teach the law-breaker a lesson and to warn other people not to ignore the rules. If there were no rules, driving would become a nightmare. If we did not enforce traffic laws, driving would become increasingly unsafe—and so would walking. We need to limit everyone's freedom so that all of us can use the road. No sensible person would want it any other way.

Who Sets the Limits

Limits are necessary in all areas of life. We can't have a society without them. In fact, we wouldn't be very reliable people if we didn't set them for ourselves. The need for limits creates the odd situation called a *paradox*. Limits make you want to be free—but freedom without any limits soon stops being freedom. To grow up properly, we need to learn to balance freedom with reasonable limits. How well we manage to do that becomes a real test of our maturity.

In each country the government sets the rules and limits what people are permitted to do. Police, law courts, fines, and prison cells make sure most people obey. When it comes to modern Judaism, however, there are no such enforcements. In contemporary society everyone is free to be religious or not, as they choose. Although people may try to influence you or persuade you to act or believe as they do, no one can legally force you to do what you don't believe. Yet even Reform Judaism, which teaches the great importance of personal freedom, has tried to give Reform Jews a sense of the limits they should set for their Jewish freedom.

In the early days of Reform Judaism, people didn't have to ask about the limits of their freedom. Reform seemed so sensible in showing how to get away from the ghetto and still stay Jewish. As a result, almost all Reform congregations conducted services largely in English, began and ended each service with a hymn, and acted very formal. That simply seemed the right thing to do.

In recent years, people have become less certain that there is only one way to modernize Judaism. While some have sought to be "more Jewish," others have chosen to break radically with Jewish tradition. The extremes made people ask if there are any limits to what Reform Jews are free to do.

Probably the most distressing question has been intermarriage. Should Reform rabbis marry a Jew to someone who isn't Jewish? The rabbis who perform such ceremonies say that they are trying to save the large number of Jews who are marrying out of Judaism. They believe that they are "keeping the door open" to Judaism for the intermarried couple and their future children instead of chasing them away. The majority of Reform rabbis feels that these rabbis are not using their freedom wisely. They said this to their colleagues in a formal vote of the Central Conference of American Rabbis. But that raised another issue: Do some Reform Jews have the right to tell others what to do?

There are rabbis who are willing to co-officiate with a minister or a priest. A number of them do so at weddings being held in churches. A few will even say a blessing at a marriage that is part of a Catholic mass where communion is taken. The overwhelming majority of Reform rabbis thinks such acts show a lack of Jewish self-respect. Doing so certainly seems to say that one might just as well be Christian as Jewish. Surely this seems to be a clear case of the abuse of freedom. Nonetheless, most Reform rabbis would rather be unhappy about the practices of the minority than try to punish them and thereby deny their freedom.

And what about the range of behavior of ordinary Jews? Take the matter of the Sabbath, which is one of the Ten Commandments. If your parents don't work on Wednesday, should you observe Shabbat then? Is eating a fancy dinner with your family on Friday night celebration enough? Perhaps Saturday is the only convenient day for you to go shopping, something you enjoy very much. Can shopping be your form of Shabbat joy? Or gymnastics competitions? Or do you feel that a "pot party" would be a truly spiritual Shabbat experience?

There is no one right answer to each of these questions for all Reform Jews. Still, the very variety of what goes on suggests that there ought to be some limits to what is acceptable. Not everything Jews do is Jewish. Not every modern experiment has to be acceptable to Reform Jews. The Reform movement doesn't want to dictate what people must or must not do. But there can be no freedom without some limits.

Setting Limits

The best kind of limits are the ones people set for themselves. For Reform Jews to set their own limits responsibly, they ought to know about Judaism. We don't often think of knowledge as a way of limiting freedom, but it's like passing the written exam for a driver's license. Unless you know the rules and restrictions, you don't belong on the road.

Belief in God, in Torah, and in Israel (the Jewish people) are basic to all Jews. Reform Jews have the freedom to form their own modern understanding of these beliefs so long as some personal sense of each of the three core beliefs underlies their Jewish life.

Let's explore how these beliefs shape a Jewish way of living. We will begin with the easiest one, the People of Israel.

We Are Not Alone

Being Jewish is not something you are all by yourself. You are part of an old and extraordinary people. Being a Jew means taking into account what other Jews do. Observing Shabbat on Thursday may give you a personal day of rest,

Caring for others is an important part of being Jewish. In Tucson, Arizona, the Jewish community sponsors a ten-kilometer run on behalf of Jews in the Soviet Union.

but it is not the Jewish Shabbat. When you celebrate it on Friday night and Saturday you know that you are joining with other Jews all around the world—and you are sharing in a celebration that Jews have carried on for over three thousand years.

A community has to agree on certain basics in order to stay together. Though we'd like to be completely free, most of us willingly accept the rule that a red light means "stop" and a green one, "go." So, too, in the Jewish community. While some people might like to regularly hold services at midnight or just as the sun begins coming up, most Jews want to have services at sundown or during the evening or mid-morning. We all have to give up some of our freedom in order to be part of a group.

As a people we can accomplish things individuals can't. Acting alone to help the victims of an earthquake or to get Jews out of the Soviet Union won't have much effect. But tens of thousands of people working together can do extraordinary things. The existence of the Jewish state adds military and political force to our numbers. Had there been a strong State of Israel during the Second World War, perhaps Hitler would never have dared to treat the Jews of Europe as he did. Sometimes we must do what our Jewish people asks us to do even though we don't prefer it, simply because we know that as a united group we can accomplish much more than each individual could possibly get done alone.

There are also special occasions when the Jewish community has to make decisions. If there is an anti-Semitic outbreak in the community, or Congress is considering a bill that will make it difficult for the State of Israel to survive, the representatives of the Jewish community must act on our behalf—and do so quickly. So, too, with specific Reform Jewish concerns. While the Reform movement cares about everyone's right to express opinions, its leaders sometimes have to take actions that not every individual Reform Jew will agree with. Even in normal times, when a vote is taken on a particular question, the decision goes according to the majority. The minority may be unhappy at the outcome but, if it was a fair debate, they will go along with the group. In that way, democratically reached decisions also limit individual freedom.

Being part of the Jewish people unquestionably limits personal freedom.

Caring to Know and Knowing to Care: the Reform Jewish Belief in Torah

---

Too many people today don't care much about religious choices. They worry more about how they will be accepted than about what they are doing. They get used to a little cheating, a little lying. After all, "everyone does it"—but not people who care about what they do with their lives.

We Jews have an excellent resource to help us become fine human beings: our Torah. By Torah, we don't mean only the first five books of the Bible. We mean the whole tradition created by sensitive Jews over the centuries in response to what they felt God "wanted" of them. Despite modernity, it is remarkable how wise many of these Jewish books remain. Indeed, when it comes to the very greatest questions—What does life mean? How ought we to live? What is our destiny?—they remain our finest guides.

Of course, not all of Torah transfers easily into our lives. We read in the Talmud that "people are forbidden to sit down to eat until they have first fed their cattle" (Ber. 40a). This hardly seems to apply to us since few of us are farmers. Yet it can still teach us about our obligations to animals and perhaps even to all life in the universe. A good Jew should be concerned about how human beings treat all living things.

Sometimes the deepest lessons come from seemingly unlikely Jewish sources. Most Reform Jews are very far from the Hasidic movement in matters of belief, practice, religious mood, and personal style. Yet Reform Jews have learned a great deal from the Hasidic interest in helping each individual grow toward God. A fine example is the story of Reb Zusya of Hanipol. He was one of the most saintly of all the Hasidim. So his disciples were very surprised that, when he was dying, they found him crying in fear. They asked him why he was so frightened. He said, "I am not worried that when I come before the Heavenly Court they may ask me, 'Zusya, why were you not like Moses?' But what will happen if they ask me, 'Zusya, why were you not truly Zusya?'"

Reform Jews need to know the Torah tradition to make intelligent decisions about it. Since it is so easy to give in to the "idols" outside or the foolish impulses within, we can benefit from measuring what we are thinking of doing against the standards of accumulated Jewish wisdom.

And What Shall We Say About God?

The last and most difficult "basic" to talk about is belief in God and how that affects the use of freedom. Most people aren't sure just what they believe, or how to explain their feelings. They are uncomfortable with the subject. It is easier to understand the fact that the Torah is holy—after all, everyone stands whenever it is taken out of the ark. But no one can see God or even imagine what God might really be like. And yet some sort of belief in God is basic to Reform Judaism.

Even America, the land of liberty, has not been free of anti-Semitic outbursts, such as this nineteenth century cartoon. Having a strong and united Jewish community is the best way to defend our freedom.

THE DREAM OF THE JEWS REALIZED.

The Reform movement created Confirmation, a ceremony for Jewish young people when they conclude their years of religious study. Although styles and curricula change over the years, today's confirmands make the same affirmation as their predecessors: a commitment to God, Torah, and the Jewish people.

It is very hard to explain God. In talking about God we must use human words. If we are not careful, God begins to sound something like the most powerful and important human being—but Jews have long known that God is too great for that. God is beyond even our very best words for God!

Ideas are easier to grasp when they are explained in terms of what people know or experience. The Bible and the prayer book speak about God as a shepherd or as king of the universe. They take it for granted that we will understand that these words are not meant literally. God doesn't really chase sheep or sit on a throne wearing a crown. These are *symbols*, words used to describe something people feel deeply but for which no one has exact terms.

When modern writers want to signal that a word is symbolic, they put quotation marks around it—and so now will we. Jewish thinkers have taught about God as the most important "force" in the universe. God "created" in order to "set" its rules. God does not "rule" the world for evil. Nor is God neutral about good and evil. God is good—which is why it is such a problem to us when there is evil in the world.

Most important, God has "made" people capable of knowing the good and doing it. The best way to be good is by listening to one's own conscience. And the best way of not confusing conscience with other notions of what may be right is by building a close personal relationship with God. That's what the religious life is all about—staying close to God so that each of us will have a strong sense of the right way to live and the courage to live that way. Most people, despite their questions and confusions about what they believe, can accept some form of these ideas about God. And having some personal sense of what is most important in the universe—God—they will try to live their lives as God would "want" them to.

How does this come into our lives? In our sensitive moods, we often feel that we are not utterly alone in the universe. There is *something* far greater than us that shaped the world and made it possible for us to be part of it. Sometimes we get this sense when we look at the grandeur of nature—a craggy mountain, the ocean, a lightning storm, the starry sky. Sometimes the feeling comes in moments of quietness—early in the morning, when the world seems still to be asleep; or when we look at the delicate petals of a flower; or hear a bird singing in a tree. The birth of a baby is a wonder; the ability to laugh is a surprising gift; the power in talent and creativity is a miracle. Seeing someone ease another person's hurt can move us very deeply. Feeling inside ourselves the strong urge for justice helps us know that we are God-like. But it is when we love deeply, most of all, that we sense the greatest Power that runs through all of creation.

Religious people, for all their doubts, know that their lives are involved with an Other as close to them as it is mysterious, as involved with them as it is radically greater than they can ever be. And they know that this Other is

We can experience a sense of God's presence through the beauty of nature and the work of human creativity.

the source of their sense of goodness and the test of their staying true to it. Being faithful to the Other, to the best of their ability to build a relationship with it, is the basis of their lives. They know that there is no more important thing they can do, for everything else in life will flow from it.

Something like this religious understanding seems to be at the heart of the freedom Reform Jews have to think about God. Reform Jews will best use their freedom not as if they were all that counted in this world, but in terms of what they believe about God. And being Jews, they will act on their beliefs in line with the Jewish people's ongoing relationship with God. Over the centuries, this Jewish closeness to God has produced the Torah-tradition. Caring Jews today have the obligation to continue and develop that tradition.

Our God, our group, our tradition—all three will influence us as we make our choices and build our lives. If we care about nothing much beyond ourselves we will not be very good Jews. But the more we care about God, Torah, and Israel (the Jewish people), the more deeply Jewish our lives will be. These concerns are the limits that must be placed on Reform Jewish freedom.

CHAPTER NINE

Organizations of Reform Judaism

Your family belongs to a synagogue and, in a way, that is a considerable burden. You pay dues and, possibly, school fees and building fund pledges as well. You may make High Holiday contributions and contributions to special temple funds. On top of all that, your parents are asked to serve on committees, help out at functions, and attend fund raisers. They occasionally complain about all the demands the temple makes on them. Yet they continue to belong and probably continue to work. Why do they bother?

Why do Reform Jews, who are free to determine their own practice, need synagogues in the first place? Why can't each Reform Jew simply be a good Jew at home, in school, at work, and with friends?

The simplest answer is that, in America, the synagogue is the most important Jewish place for most of its members.

But there's another, more complicated answer. Many Jewish activities work best when lots of people take part; some wouldn't happen at all without the support of a congregation. That's because our religion concerns the Jewish people as a whole, as well as each of us as individuals. Take a look at the prayer book. Almost every prayer and blessing talks about "our" God and what "we" should do or what "we" hope will happen to "us."

Each congregation develops its own style. How would you describe the style of your congregation?

For all their personal freedom, Reform Jews work together as an organized group in Judaism. The smallest unit is the synagogue. Choosing to belong to a synagogue immediately places limits on the freedom of individual members. Each congregation develops a style that makes most of its members feel comfortable. The service may contain a lot of Hebrew or a little. There may be sermons only or also open discussions. There may be a feeling of warmth and informality in the synagogue, or a sense of grandeur and awesomeness.

Individual Reform Jews can choose to belong to the congregation that best suits their needs but they cannot insist that every decision the congregation makes will follow their taste. Sometimes, people who have helped set the style of a synagogue in its early days discover that newer members are introducing many changes. The mood of that temple is no longer what made its founders love it. Some of them may leave; others will learn to live with the changes. A temple "grows" and "develops" as a person does. Belonging to a congregation over the years means being part of a changing community. Most Reform Jews are willing to accept the demands that this makes on their personal freedom.

The Person on the Pulpit

Have you ever wondered about how your rabbi got to be a rabbi, and why he or she became the rabbi of your congregation?

Your rabbi spent five years after finishing college learning the things a rabbi needs to know. Actually, most of the courses at the rabbinical school would be suitable for anyone who wanted to be a learned Jew. Except for performing weddings, which are controlled by state law, Jewish teaching says that everything rabbis do can be done by any well-educated Jew. Only most of us would rather leave such intensive Jewish study to the people who choose to work as rabbis. We make the rabbi our Jewish specialist, and in this way, too, we give up some of our freedom.

Reform rabbis need to know not only about Judaism but also about human affairs, about working with people, about helping them in times of crisis, about how we can make our communities and society better, and very much more besides. Such complex training couldn't possibly be afforded by each congregation for itself. That's why the congregations of the Reform movement joined together to have a first-rate rabbinical school.

Sometimes the mood and look of a congregation can change over the years. The photographs show the old and new buildings of Temple Mount Sinai, in El Paso, Texas.

Training Jewish Professionals: HUC-JIR

The Reform movement's seminary for training rabbis is called Hebrew Union College-Jewish Institute of Religion (HUC-JIR). It has this long name because it is the merger of two great rabbinical schools, and no one wanted either of the original schools to be forgotten. HUC, the older and larger of the two, was located in Cincinnati, Ohio; JIR was in New York City. HUC-JIR still has campuses in both locations and more recent ones in Los Angeles, California, and in Jerusalem, Israel. These campuses and their many activities are supported by all the Reform congregations together.

Not all Reform rabbis have been ordained by HUC-JIR. Your rabbi may have grown up in another country and studied, instead, at the Leo Baeck College in London, the Reform movement's international training school for rabbis. Or your rabbi may have studied at an Orthodox or Conservative rabbinical seminary, or at the Reconstructionist Rabbinical College and come into the Reform movement later on. Ask him/her and find out.

Once a rabbi has been ordained and is looking for a pulpit, no one can force that rabbi on a congregation, and no one can force a rabbi to stay. If the rabbi and congregation aren't happy with one another, the rabbi applies for another position and the congregation then interviews the rabbis who are interested in filling that pulpit.

Most Reform rabbis receive their training at HUC-JIR. This photograph was taken at ordination services at the Isaac Mayer Wise Temple in Cincinnati.

The CCAR — Organization for Rabbis

The organization that helps congregations find the right rabbi to serve them is called the Central Conference of American Rabbis (CCAR). It is the national organization of Reform rabbis and it carries on many activities individual rabbis cannot do by themselves.

For example, the official Reform prayer books have been published by the CCAR. Some years ago, when many rabbis and congregations were unhappy with the prayer book they had been using, they asked the CCAR to begin the process of issuing a new prayer book. That started a long, complicated chain of events. First, the CCAR committee on prayer prepared sample services to see what might best express the contemporary religious mood. Some rabbis and congregations asked for more Hebrew and traditional readings; some wanted modern English instead of a style that sounded old-fashioned. Others wanted the State of Israel and the Holocaust reflected in the prayers. Still others requested services that talked of God as a power in the universe rather than in the traditional terms (king, father, shepherd, etc.).

The committee worked hard for a number of years and came up with more trial services. Finally, a "draft" of the new prayer book was sent to each of the more than twelve hundred members of the CCAR. The rabbis were asked for their opinions on the services, for changes and corrections in the wording, and for the reactions of congregants who used the services. The resulting volume for Shabbat, festivals, and weekdays is called *Gates of Prayer* (in Hebrew, *Shaarei Tefilah*). It contains ten different *erev Shabbat* services and six Sabbath morning services, as well as weekday and festival services and additional readings for special occasions. A High Holy Day *mahzor* (called *Gates of Repentance* or *Shaarei Teshuvah*) and a home prayer book (*Gates of the House* or *Shaarei Habayit*) have also been published.

These prayer books were the work of very many members of the Central Conference of American Rabbis. No single rabbi or even small group of rabbis could have accomplished such a great task. These books provide congregations with options that they may not have realized they wanted when they first requested a change. In this case, giving up local freedom has provided the benefits that result from a group effort.

When *Gates of Prayer* was offered for sale, no one *had* to buy it. Some Reform congregations preferred to continue using the previous prayer book, while others decided to continue experimenting with their own creative services. But the overwhelming majority of congregations has chosen the new prayer book. Not everyone who uses *Gates of Prayer* is happy with it, in spite of the wide variety of services. Still, the prayer book does satisfy so many people in so many congregations that we can say it speaks to the needs of Reform Jews, at least for the present.

The Union

Some things are done not just by scholars or rabbis but by the Reform movement as a whole. Congregations and rabbis cooperate together in our biggest organization, the Union of American Hebrew Congregations (UAHC). By bringing all the energies of Reform Jews together, the Union can do all kinds of projects that no congregation could do on its own.

The Union's headquarters are located on Fifth Avenue in New York City. It is an interesting place to visit when you take a trip to New York. Synagogue Activities, Social Action, College Youth—just reading the names of the various departments on the bulletin board in the lobby is very impressive. And then there are the Union's camps around the country. Have you been to Harlam or Eisner or Swig or Oconomowoc? At these camps, young people can get together and enjoy a whole range of informal activities in a Reform Jewish framework. The Kutz camp, in Warwick, N.Y., is dedicated solely to leadership and study programs for high school students from all over North America.

The North American Federation of Temple Youth (NFTY) supervises the Union's high school program. Each UAHC region has its own subdivision of NFTY, and within the region each congregation has its own youth group. (What are the initials of your region?) Your synagogue's senior youth group not only runs its own meetings and events, but also participates in the special activities planned for the region: conclaves, study seminars, dances, work programs, song and dance institutes, and weekends at the nearest Union camp.

The Union's Youth Department sponsors summer trips to Israel, work-study programs, and exchange student opportunities. There is a College Youth division, which organizes Reform Jewish activities on many campuses around the country.

The National Federation of Temple Brotherhoods (NFTB) and the National Federation of Temple Sisterhoods (NFTS) are the parent organizations of each congregation's own brotherhood and sisterhood. They give suggestions and help with programming, and share ideas for fund raising. NFTS helps support HUC-JIR and has, among other worthy projects, contributed community buildings at Kibbutz Yahel, the first Reform kibbutz in Israel. NFTB's Jewish Chautauqua Society sponsors rabbis to lecture on Judaism at colleges throughout the country. It also fights prejudice by giving these schools some basic books about Judaism and makes films for the general public that present a positive understanding of Jewish life.

In Union There is Strength

Through the Union, Reform congregations have a powerful shared way of making the voice of Reform Judaism heard by the rest of the world. But how can the Union speak for all of its members? Doesn't that take away the personal freedom of individual Reform Jews and individual Reform congregations?

The Union arrives at the positions it takes by the democratic process. Each member congregation sends some of its leaders as delegates to a huge, exciting Biennial Assembly, a five-day gathering that occurs every two years. There, Reform Jewish leaders from across the continent meet, compare congregational activities, share problems, study Judaism, and form friendships. In committee meetings and when the whole assembly gathers, the delegates study and discuss resolutions prepared by a UAHC committee, or by one or more congregations, or by a UAHC region or group of regions.

Many years ago, young children—particularly from immigrant and other poor families—were put to work in factories for long hours. They had no chance to go to school or to play. They not only grew up uneducated but emotionally and physically damaged. Through its resolutions, the Union spoke out forcefully against child labor and, with other groups, helped to get laws passed preventing the exploitation of children.

Union resolutions have dealt with moral issues here and abroad: desegregation, apartheid, genocide, energy, strategic arms limitation, and refugee policies, to name a very few. They have been concerned with congregational practices—like objecting to gambling as a means of congregational fund raising or moving Confirmation from the ninth to the tenth grade. In recent years, women's rights have received considerable attention as has Reform's need to reach people outside the traditional family "norm": young singles, unmarried adults, the divorced, widows and widowers, the single-parent family, and intermarried couples.

Some resolutions are fiercely debated, with many delegates taking their turn at microphones to persuade others to vote along with them. Other resolutions have passed almost unanimously, because they express the outlook of most of the delegates (who, of course, are themselves speaking for their congregations). After a resolution has been passed by a majority vote, it becomes the official position of the Reform movement on that subject. Between Biennials, the Union's Board of Trustees governs the Union's day-to-day operations, following guidelines set by earlier Biennial resolutions.

Must a Reform congregation or an individual Reform Jew feel bound by these resolutions? No. Individual freedom remains—but the majority has ruled. Obviously, in continuing to disagree, a thoughtful Reform Jew will weigh the reasons that led the majority at a Biennial to decide as it did. After all, Judaism is more than an individual matter: Jews have always worked together as a community. By joining together in local congregations and their great Union, individual Reform Jews join themselves to the Reform movement and the Jewish people.

Freedom vs. Union

Is there a contradiction between personal Reform Jewish freedom and the UAHC speaking as the "united voice" of Reform Jews? Not if you believe in democracy. Having freedom cannot mean always acting alone. It surely includes joining with other people who are committed both to freedom and to Judaism. Sometimes that will mean having to give in for the sake of the group. Since it is not always clear when it is wise to do so, groups have fights. You have probably had that experience in your own family, and most congregations go through that as well.

Fortunately, the Reform movement has a pretty good record of people being willing to make compromises with one another. When people really care about their own freedom they respect other people's freedom and will make great efforts to learn to work with them.

The love of freedom got Reform Judaism started on the process of modernizing Judaism in the first place. But it is very hard to balance the drive for freedom with a sense of Jewish group responsibility in order to be at the same time free individuals and loyal Jews. Your synagogue and the organizations of the Reform movement will guide you in achieving that sort of Jewish freedom. Using it wisely will be the best sign that you are becoming a mature Reform Jew.

PART THREE

What Do Reform Jews Believe?

Three basic beliefs unite all Jews: faith in God, the acceptance of Torah, and allegiance to the Jewish people. "Israel, Torah, and the Holy One blessed be God are one" is how a very old saying expresses it. Everyone who identifies him/herself as a Jew is asserting a connection with all three of these concepts.

As you have already begun to see, there are many different interpretations of what each one means. In this section, we will examine more closely the special Reform Jewish understandings of God, the Jewish People, and Torah.

CHAPTER TEN

About God

People have always used symbolic language to help them explain their thoughts and feelings about God. How else could they talk about God? After all, we have no contact with God through our senses. We cannot literally feel, see, smell, taste, or hear our God. So good Jews cannot make statues or idols of our God. God is greater than anything inside or outside nature—but we do the best we can. As one Sage, Rabbi Ishmael, explained: "the Torah speaks in the language of ordinary people."

That is why descriptions of God have often sounded as if God were a person. The Torah says God has an "outstretched arm," a "face" that "shines," eyes, ears, nose, and mouth. God "walks" in the Garden of Eden. Giving God human characteristics is called anthropomorphism (from the Greek root *anthropo* meaning "human being," *morph* meaning "form" or "shape," and *ism* meaning "system"). Anthropopathism means giving God human feelings—like love, hate, anger, jealousy, rage, despair, sadness, or forgiveness. People have been comfortable with such images because human beings can relate to them so completely. They personalize God. But Jews have always recognized these images as symbols and understood that God is truly grander than anything we might ever imagine.

The artist Michelangelo, in his painting on the ceiling of the Sistine Chapel, depicts God in human terms.

Does God Change?

One reason that there are so many different kinds of symbols for God is because people's ideas about God have changed over the years. The language changes, but Jews realize it continues to describe the same God.

When Jews learned Greek philosophy, they spoke of God very differently from the way the Bible had. Philo, a Jewish thinker of the first century C.E.,

Pagans imagined their gods as male or female, human or animal. By contrast, Jews have always believed that God is beyond imagining.

talked of God as "Pure Spirit." More than a thousand years later, Maimonides said God was "Pure Thought."

The Jewish mystics had still other ways of thinking about God. In the Zohar (written about 1275 C.E.), God is called *ein sof*—"without limits"—so pure and exalted that nothing at all can properly be said about God. But mystics also say God can be described in terms of *sefirot*, ten "centers of power" that can be talked about in everyday language.

After the Emancipation, many Jews began studying at the universities and came into contact with modern philosophy. Of course, their understanding of God then began changing. Let us see how it gave them a new interpretation of the belief that God is one.

A beautiful reading in *Gates of Prayer* says, "Days pass and the years vanish, and we walk sightless among miracles." And another suggests, "Were the sun to rise but once a year, we would all cry out: How great are Your works O God, and how glorious! Our hymns would rise up, our thanks would ascend. O God, Your wonders are endless, yet we do not see!"

We take so much for granted. The workings of nature, the fact that our bodies normally function so marvelously, the very fact that we are alive. These should be our proof of God. Yet it is only when things go wrong that most people look for God—and then often to question God's existence and fairness.

The Problem of Evil

The need to find new ideas continues because our minds and sensibilities expand—and so, too, do our questions and doubts. Why are there floods or devastating earthquakes? Why is it that good people seem to suffer while so many rotten people are thriving? Can we explain the death of a little child or a beloved parent as punishment? Or accept it as an orderly happening? Why is there evil in the world?

There are no easy answers to any of these questions. The problem of evil has bothered Jews since biblical days. Abraham pleaded with God to spare Sodom and Gomorrah for the sake of the few good people who might be living in the cities. He asked, "Should not the judge of all the earth deal justly?" Moses was upset by the way the Hebrew slaves were suffering, and complained to God, "O Eternal One, why did You bring harm upon this people? Why did You send me? Ever since I came to Pharaoh to speak in Your name, it has gone worse with this people; yet You have not delivered Your people at all" (Ex. 5:22-23). Jeremiah cried out because he could not understand why God must punish the entire people of Israel so severely. And the Hasidic master, Rabbi Levi Yitzhak from Berditchev, challenged God's treatment of the Jews and told God to judge God's own actions according to the laws of Torah.

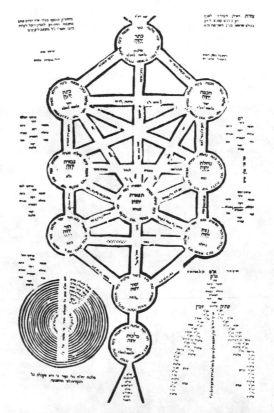

A diagram of the Ten Sefirot, or centers of God's power according to Kabbalistic thought.

Modern Jews now have added another problem to this heavy list: the Holocaust. Where was God then? Some Jewish thinkers have said flatly that this tragedy to our people proves that God is dead. Others have tried to explain how God could have permitted six million Jews to die. For help they turned to the Bible. The Biblical writers talk about God's nearness as "seeing God's face." And they describe the worst moments in their history, times when God seemed to have deserted them, as times when God's "face," so to speak, was "hidden" from the Jews. What was true then has been true in our time. For reasons we do not know, God is sometimes very close. For reasons we also do not know—but suffer from greatly—God sometimes seems utterly absent. But as our ancestors trusted, so will we. And we say, symbolically, God's "face" was "hidden" in the days of the death camps. A Jew hiding from the Nazis wrote these words on the wall in a cellar in Cologne, Germany: "I believe in the sun even when it is not shining. I believe in love even when I do not feel it. I believe in God even when God is silent."

Some creative thinkers have suggested that we should now think of God as limited in power—finite rather than infinite. God does all the good God can. But God, too, can't do everything. According to this view, God needs human beings in order for God to grow and become perfect. God "grows" with human goodness. But this view has difficulty dealing with the possibility that a limited God might some day stop growing, or even be unable, with human help, to defeat the forces of evil.

Our Jewish thinkers have not settled for only one idea about God. They

Although we sometimes call the synagogue the House of God, we do not mean that God actually lives there. It is the place where we join together as a community to renew our faith and to try to understand what God expects of us.

continue to question and to search. Reform Judaism encourages this activity. The process of questioning is another important aspect of Reform Jewish freedom. New ideas help re-form Judaism so that new generations of Jews can continue to live comfortably as Jews in the modern world.

Life After Death

Human beings have always been curious about whether there is any sort of life after death. For a long time, Jews had faith in some kind of existence that continued beyond death. They believed that "at the end of days" a complete return to life—a physical resurrection miraculously brought about by God—would take place. Other Jews believed that there are two components to a human being, the physical body and the spiritual "soul." After the body dies, the soul survives.

Later, science began describing human beings in chemical terms. But if people are only chemical matter, what "lives on"? Early Reform Jews were impressed with these scientific discoveries. Actual life after death now seemed like an impossible notion. But ideas about the "soul" or "spirit" as separate from the "flesh" spoke of something about people that seemed more than chemical—and so the most precious part of each human being could survive death. Other Reform Jews said that the dead become immortal by living on in the memories of the people who loved them and in their good deeds.

Many Reform Jews have held on to a belief in life after death because there is so much that is mysterious about life itself. Does science really understand everything about human beings' ability to think and feel? Why should we deny that, just as life holds mysteries, there are possibilities in the mystery we know as death? If there is some kind of ultimate reward and punishment, or divine justice, it becomes easier to live with the evil that exists in our world. Is the attractiveness of the idea enough reason to believe in it? The answer depends on how much we feel we can trust God. Having seen all the benefits God has given us as we live, shouldn't we expect the same goodness when we die? God is the Creator of death as well as of life. If life serves God's good purposes, should we not have faith that death will do the same?

These are hard ideas even to *think* about, and we cannot be sure of answers to any of them. It should be comforting to know that Reform Judaism does not try to stifle such questions. It encourages them, in the hope that better answers will be revealed. There is room for searching in Judaism, as Reform Jews understand Judaism, and the belief that we must try to grow despite all our doubts.

This means that you, too, are free to question and to doubt as you find your own way to God. Whether by thinking or by feeling, perhaps you will find a way for us all to better understand God.

CHAPTER ELEVEN

About the Jewish People

If you were to ask everyone in your class to say what makes a person Jewish, you'd probably get many different answers. You might be told that a Jew is someone who goes to synagogue, or doesn't celebrate Christmas, or believes in one God, or supports the State of Israel, or eats chicken soup (or blintzes, or gefilte fish, etc.). That's an odd collection of identifications. Being Jewish obviously isn't a simple matter.

There are many people who proudly say they are Jews, but never even go into a synagogue, except perhaps—and then only sometimes—on Yom Kippur.

And not celebrating Christian holidays only makes one not Christian, or not an observant Christian. Moslems don't celebrate Christmas either. They certainly aren't Jews.

There are also Jews who say they do not believe in God at all yet still consider themselves Jewish. Whether to escape from the shtetl-type closeness that was choking them or to embrace modern culture and science, they spurn religious belief. Even some rabbis claim that there is no God and point to the Holocaust as evidence. Faith in one God, therefore, isn't the key to being Jewish either.

90

All these people are Jewish, yet each speaks a different language and exhibits a different style of dress. What do they have in common?

And are there really Jewish foods? If you were to look carefully through an international cookbook you'd discover that most of what people think of as Jewish foods are actually adaptations of Russian or Hungarian or German dishes—the foods of the countries in which Jews were living. Sephardic Jewish foods are totally different from Ashkenazic ones and resemble the cuisine of North Africa, Greece, and other Mediterranean countries. The same is true of Jewish music and Jewish dances. So eating certain foods or dancing the hora doesn't make one Jewish.

The United States government supports the State of Israel. Therefore, caring about Israel's welfare doesn't make people Jewish either. And Israel itself, the "Jewish State," where religion and government aren't separate, nevertheless doesn't have rabbis running the country. As a matter of fact, most Israeli Jews don't even belong to synagogues. They say that they are Jewish, but not religious. Being Jewish is obviously a complex affair.

Is Judaism a Religion?

Perhaps we should approach the issue differently. In this country, people talk about Judaism as one of the "three great religions." If someone asks what your religion is, you may wonder why they want to know but you have no question about the answer: you are Jewish. We normally identify Judaism as a religion.

And with good reason. Our families belong to a synagogue. We attend services on Shabbat and holidays. We use books of prayer and blessings at our services. We keep precious Torah scrolls in a holy ark, and have a light always burning in the sanctuary to remind us of God's eternal presence. At the appropriate seasons we light candles, have a *seder*, perhaps build a *sukkah*. All are part of our celebration of Jewish religious holidays.

So Judaism is a religion. But what about those Jews who don't believe in God? And what do language, food, or country have to do with religion? Is there a Protestant homeland? Or Catholic foods? Or a Methodist language or atheist Baptists or secular Mormons? Do you see the problem? Simply defining Judaism as a religion doesn't explain many of the things that are very much part of Judaism and of being Jewish.

Take our history. All Jews share a four thousand-year-old history. It stretches from Bible times through the Roman and Babylonian periods, into the "golden age" in Spain and the migration of Jews throughout the world. It includes our tragic loss in the Holocaust and our rejoicing at the existence of Israel. There is no parallel to this in Christianity.

For that matter, look at the Bible, our holiest book. It doesn't even have a word for "religion"! The Bible talks about the Jews—called Hebrews, or Is-

We share the same holidays, although we don't all observe them in the same way. This Reform "Sukkah mobile" travels around Kansas City, Missouri, giving Jews an opportunity to share in the mitzvah of lulav and etrog.

raelites—in the same way it talks about the other "nations" of the Middle East, like the Amalekites, Philistines, or Moabites.

Each of these peoples had its own language, its own territory, its own history, and usually a religion of some sort. Sometimes they were independent and had their own kings. Sometimes they lived as a group within the territory of a more powerful nation. The Jews fit into this pattern too.

One thing made the Jewish folk different. They believed that one God ruled over the entire universe, and they continued to worship God wherever they lived. By contrast, the other nations gave up their own gods and adopted the gods of their conquerors, or combined the old and new together in an attempt to satisfy everyone.

So the Jews were a unique religious group in Bible times. And yet, even then, they were more than only a religion.

Are We a Nation?

Since the Bible treats the Jews the way it treats the other nations, then perhaps the Jews are a nation. Yet what kind of nation exists without a country? For almost half of Jewish history, the vast majority of Jews has lived away from Israel, with virtually no possibility of returning there. Hebrew had stopped being the national language. For a while, Jews spoke Aramaic. Later, they spoke Judeo-Arabic, or Yiddish, or the language of the countries in which they lived.

However, Hebrew did not die out. It continued as the language of study and prayer. Love for the Jewish homeland was not lost either. Prayers for a return to Jerusalem were part of the daily worship services of pious Jews. The last line of the Passover Haggadah says "next year in Jerusalem." Israel remained "home" for Jews, in their hearts if not in their lives.

Another reminder of continuing Jewish ties to Israel has been the calendar. Jewish holidays all follow a calendar whose year begins in Tishri, on Rosh Hashanah.

Wherever in the world they live, all Jews celebrate Tu b'Shevat—the New Year of the Trees—at the time when young saplings are being planted in Israel. The cold weather has ended—there. In many other parts of the world, however, it is still winter. The ground is frozen and covered with snow. It is certainly not spring for Jews living in those places. And it is late summer for the Jews of South America and Australia. Yet Jews all around the world continue to mark the arrival of spring in Israel. Some people have said that the practice of eating fruits from Israel on Tu b'Shevat—figs, dates, carobs, or oranges, very expensive and hard to come by in the years before refrigerated railroad cars and airplanes—kept the Land of Israel alive in Jewish hearts over the centuries.

Observing holidays at the "wrong" time of year makes sense when we understand that the observance is in itself a reminder of Jewish ties to Israel, the Jewish "national home." The modern State of Israel has provided a focus for this strong sense of Jewish "nationalism."

"Nation" Problems in America

Jewish nationalism was a problem for many Jews in the years following the Emancipation. When Reform Jews first came to America from Germany in the nineteenth century, they were eager to adapt Judaism to their new surroundings. They had learned from the experience of Jews in Western Europe that governments would accept them only as individual members of a "religion" and not as a unified national group. It seemed illogical for the citizens of one

Many Reform Jews have contributed time and money to the Zionist cause. This stock certificate, for shares in the Jewish homeland, was purchased in 1900 by members of a Reform congregation in Baltimore, Maryland.

nation to belong at the same time to another nation. People with dual loyalty would be treasonous to one if they supported the other—and perhaps unfaithful to both if they supported neither one.

So most Reform Jews in America minimized the "national" parts of Judaism. Where possible, they used Christianity as their model and they created a way of being Jewish and American that kept their tradition alive in a new social setting. For example, they conducted their services largely in English, with great solemnity and no longer mentioned "returning" to Israel in their prayers.

The Pittsburgh Platform of 1885 said very specifically that it made no sense for American Jews to continue observing laws designed for people living in ancient Israel. They did not long for a king descended from King David. Nor did they want to see the ancient Temple rebuilt or have a priestly cult again offer animal sacrifices. So they dropped the old prayers for the Messiah and instead focused their attention on America, which seemed to them the land of promise.

However, at the very time that Reform Jews were emphasizing complete loyalty to the country where they made their home, other Jews began a movement to rebuild the Land of Israel and create a political Jewish state there. This Zionist call for a Jewish homeland sounded to many Reformers like disloyalty to America. They were afraid it would jeopardize their freedom in America, so they argued against it.

Not all Reform Jews agreed with these fears. Reform rabbis like Stephen

Stephen S. Wise, the prominent Reform rabbi who founded the Jewish Institute of Religion, was outspoken in his support for Zionism.

Wise and Abba Hillel Silver were among the most important and influential leaders of the Zionist movement in America. They understood that the "national" aspects were part of what made Judaism special. They already saw what we have no question about today: An American Jew can love Israel and work for Israel's security without being a traitor to his/her country. By the 1930s, the increasing dangers to the Jewish people in Europe and a better understanding of the goals of political Zionism convinced many other Reform Jews that being a Zionist didn't conflict with being a good American or weaken loyalty to Reform Judaism.

We Are a People

In recent years, it has become easy for almost every Jew to take pride in the "national" part of being Jewish. The State of Israel provides one reason. It has developed in wonderful ways, despite all its problems. Another reason is a change in American attitudes about being American. The United States used to be described as a "melting pot" into which every group's ethnic characteristics were poured. The result was a new product, a kind of all-American stew.

But people did not wish to give up the special parts of their heritage. Most American citizens are proud of their ethnic roots. A new image describes our country as an orchestra, or as a bowl of salad. In an orchestra the different instruments help each other make beautiful music. When you prepare a fruit salad, you take many kinds of fruit and blend them together to create a delicious dish. The whole is made up of parts that keep their own individual characteristics. In society this is called pluralism—it allows each ethnic group to be unique and at the same time cooperate with one another.

The phrase "ethnic group" is more acceptable today than "nation," even though *ethnos* (which gives us "ethnic") means nation. It somehow sounds

Rabbi Abba Hillel Silver (third from right) presented the case for an independent Jewish state to the United Nations General Assembly in 1947.

very unpatriotic and anti-American to talk about people of the Chinese "nation" when you mean Americans of Chinese ancestry. When you mention "ethnicity," on the other hand, everyone understands that you are referring to the pride that people take in the special characteristics of their group. And the difference is more than just a change of language. It is the mark of an important change in attitude.

Americans of Italian descent, for example, share with each other the special customs, language, food styles, culture, and history of Italy. At the same time, they are loyal Americans. They may never even have visited Italy and know only a few words in Italian. The "flavor" of their ethnic tradition, taught to them by their parents and grandparents, can contribute greatly to the richness of American culture and be enjoyed by people of other backgrounds. Just think of all the foods we love that have an Italian ethnic origin.

If shared history, language, and customs are the definition of an ethnic group, then the Jews are an ethnic group—a people. But we are an unusual ethnic group because we also have a religion. This mix of ethnicity and religion can be seen not only in the odd combination of ways we have for *being* Jewish but in the ways for *becoming* Jewish as well.

How One Becomes a Jew

Just about everything we belong to has entrance requirements. There are two ways of becoming a Jew. One is birth—being born into a Jewish family. The other is conversion. If you think about it, the combination is somewhat odd. One way has to do with who your parents are. We could call that the "national" way.

The other, the "religious" way, has to do with what you believe. If your mother converted to Judaism you are a Jew because you were born to a Jewish mother, even though she herself didn't start out being born Jewish. In that case, you inherited your Jewishness from someone who got hers through conversion. But if your father is Jewish, Reform Jews consider you a Jew even if your mother never converted to Judaism, so long as you are being raised as a Jew, go to religious school, and complete your formal Jewish education by being confirmed.

In most ways, conversion is a religious event. The very word "conversion" means a change of religious beliefs. The "declaration of faith" is a religious act. *Mikveh* and circumcision are religious rituals.

Yet becoming a Jew is also like becoming a citizen of a country. You get citizenship either by birth or by naturalization. The process of naturalization is somewhat like conversion. You study about the laws and history of your adopted country and then, in an official ceremony, agree to become a loyal, patriotic, law-abiding member of that country. Naturalized citizens accept the history and the heroes of the new country as their own, and most try to adopt its traditions and way of life. Children of naturalized Americans are American citizens by birth.

A person who is born Jewish remains a Jew forever, unless that person specifically converts to another religion. Even then, a former Jew who wishes to return to Judaism is welcomed back. That is not the case with Christianity. Christians are not born into any particular church. Many denominations, in fact, believe that their children aren't even Christian before baptism. They consider someone who leaves the church as a "heathen," no longer Christian at all.

A *Religious People*

Strangely enough, the chief problem of how to define Judaism may lie with Christianity. We live in a country that is predominantly Christian. So, too, are the European countries from which most of our families originally came. In comparison to Christian religious models, Judaism's combination of national and ethnic qualities seems strange, perhaps even unique. However, the real truth is that most religions in the world do not function merely as "churches." It is Christianity which is unusual.

Look at the entry for Islam, or Sikhs in your encyclopedia. Read about the way Sikhs integrate their "religious" beliefs with their "national" existence. You may be surprised to see how similar they are to the Jews' mixture of faith and people. If the word "religion" is inadequate to describe what these combinations actually are it is because our language has been shaped by Christianity and not because Judaism is so radically different from the other great religions of the world.

God and the Jewish people are two of the central components of our faith. We will look at the third, Torah, in the next chapter.

CHAPTER TWELVE

About the Torah, the Bible and Jewish Tradition

According to the *Guinness Book of World Records*, more than 2.5 billion copies of the Bible have been printed. Parts of the Bible have been translated into 1,710 languages and the entire Bible can be read in at least 275 languages. The Bible is today the world's most widely distributed book, as it always has been.

Certain poems, plays, stories, music, and art have remained important to people centuries after they were written and in countries far different from the ones where they originated. They continue to be popular because the people who created them were geniuses whose talents were far greater than everyone else's. Scientists like Galileo and Einstein fit into this category. So do leaders like Lincoln or thinkers like Plato. And everyone has heard of Shakespeare, Mozart, and Picasso.

Yet their accomplishments, for all their greatness, do not equal that of the Bible. People do not have "faith" in these other works of genius, or base their very lives on them, or look to them for inspiration in times of trouble or unhappiness. The Bible is special.

Who Wrote the Bible?

The Torah says that Moses wrote down all of the words God spoke at Mt. Sinai. Every one of the Torah's words—even every one of its letters— is, therefore, holy. And since God is greater by far than any human genius could be, if God wrote the Torah it must be the greatest of all possible books.

When traditional Jews speak of the holiness of the Torah, they don't only mean the Five Books of Moses. They include the rest of the Bible and all the books, like the Talmud and Midrash, that are known as the Oral Law. Traditional Jews believe that these are all sacred writings whose teachings come from God and must be obeyed.

Reform Jews agree that the Torah is the greatest of all books, but do not believe that God wrote the Bible. Here are some of their reasons.

There are a number of contradictions in the Bible and there are different versions of the Bible stories. For example, according to the Torah, the Ten Commandments were the only words God spoke directly to the people. Hence, they are particularly holy and special. Since everyone was supposedly present and heard them, there shouldn't be any question about exactly what was said. Yet the reasons for observing Shabbat are not the same in the two different parts of the Torah where the Ten Commandments appear. In the Book of Exodus, Chapter 20, the people are told to rest on Shabbat because God created the world in six days and rested on the seventh. In Deuteronomy 5, where the commandments are repeated, the fifth commandment says that people should rest on Shabbat in memory of the exodus from Egypt.

The Ten Commandments aren't the only parts of the Torah that appear in different versions. The very first event in the Bible, the story of creation, is also told in more than one way. Genesis 1:27 says, "And God created man in God's image, in the image of God was he created; male and female God created them." In the next chapter, in Genesis 2, we read that God created the first man, Adam, "from the dust of the earth." Only later, when God decided that "it is not good for man to be alone" (2:18) was the first woman created from "the rib that God had taken from the man" (2:22).

Why does the same strange encounter with a king happen twice to Sarah and Abraham, and once to Rebekkah and Isaac? Why does Jacob greet Joseph's sons with pleasure at one moment, and in the very next not even recognize them? (See Genesis 48.)

The traditional Jewish explanation for the confusions and repetitions is that every word in the Bible is there for a reason. Because God said them, they must make sense. If we can't understand them or find ways to interpret them, it is our own fault. Perhaps some answers will always remain beyond human understanding no matter how carefully the Bible continues to be analyzed and examined.

The Reform Jewish Belief About the Writing of the Bible

After the Emancipation, Jews who came into contact with modern methods of studying history and historical books found that they could not accept the idea that the Bible transmits God's own words. But if God didn't actually "speak" to Moses or the prophets, where did our ancestors get their extraordinary ideas about justice and mercy? What inspired their instructions, accepted by countless generations since, about how to live an upright and praiseworthy life? Why did the Reformers themselves continue to believe in the truth of the Bible's messages and its importance for their lives—particularly since they did not believe that God dictated it?

The Reformers looked for a modern explanation to show why the Bible was still holy. To understand the answer that satisfied them, think about the Bible's words for its creation: "And God said to Moses, 'Speak to the Israelites saying . . .'." The prophets report, "The word of God came to me" or "Thus says the Eternal One." Reform Jews came to the conclusion that when the Bible says "God spoke" it should be understood as "a religious genius sensed what God wanted."

We all know about musical geniuses who seem able to hear in ways no one else can and artistic geniuses who create beauty where others saw nothing. In religion, too, there are geniuses—individuals who are particularly sensitive to God. The biblical writers were geniuses of this sort. When a re-

Students at the New York School of HUC-JIR listen to Dean Paul Steinberg as he explains a passage from the Torah.

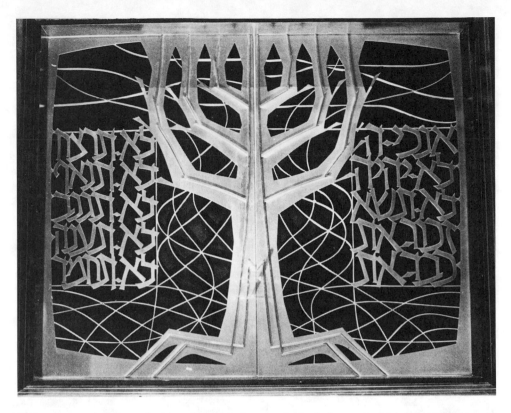

Every congregation has at least one Torah in its *aron ha-kodesh,* or ark of the law. The ark itself is often decorated with words from the Torah.

ligious inspiration came to them and they put it into a law or poem or story or history they themselves were awed by their insights and felt them too grand to be merely their own ideas. They truly believed that the very words they used came from God. Even today, when we speak of being "inspired" we are saying that what we created was greater than anything we could do alone. *In-spir-ed* literally means having a special spirit put into a person. Once in a while, everyone of us has insights greater than our normal thoughts—although most of us would hesitate to say "God told me" or claim to be religious geniuses.

An Imperfect Creation

The brilliant human beings who created the different parts of the Bible were geniuses. But they weren't perfect and they didn't have magic powers. They were people who talked in terms of what was going on in their own times. And like all people, even geniuses, they didn't know everything and they sometimes made errors. So did the people who finally put the Bible in written form. That is why sometimes letters are upside down in the Torah text or

One of these arks has an open feeling, with filigree work in metal; the other is decorated with brightly designed cloth. They are very beautiful, but what makes them important is the fact that they hold the Torah scrolls inside.

written wrongly. That is why it can say in one place that Noah should take two clean animals into the ark and in another that he should take seven.

Seeing the human factor in the Bible helps to explain why sometimes the Bible does not live up to its own high ethical standards. Our ancestors worked out the most humane laws about slavery that they could, but they didn't abolish slavery altogether. They tell the stories of Hagar and Ishmael being thrown out by Sarah, of Abraham's attempted sacrifice of Isaac, of the sale of Joseph and other acts we would consider unholy. The people who wrote and the people whose lives they told about were often inspired human beings. They were able to reach toward God in ways we cannot—and to put their insights into words more brilliantly than anyone has been able to do since their time.

Consider the ideals these writers set before us. The Bible recognizes that all human beings, not just Jews, are God's "children." It does not favor rich or famous or powerful people. It respects good people wherever they are found. The Bible calls for good societies and for countries to behave righteously. Indeed, the Bible's authors dreamt of a day when all people would live in justice and compassion, and nations would all live in peace. The Bible teaches an amazingly high standard of good and evil.

Because our ancestors were so much like the other peoples of the ancient Near East in everything else, their distinctive religious beliefs are extraordinary. Our ancestors believed in one God. They did not worship idols. They did not confuse God with any power or thing in nature, no matter how great. They knew God was mightier than whatever they could see or imagine. Although they saw confusion and conflict all around them, they continued to look for unity, harmony and peace. Despite the fact that their ideas seemed odd to others and their way of life peculiar, they knew that someday everyone would come to agree with them. They built their special sense of an invisible God into their way of life and created the distinctive Jewish way of being human and holy that Jews still accept today. No wonder that we, thousands of years later, who live in a country far different from the primitive agricultural community of old Judea, say in awe that the writers of the Bible—for all their failings—were true religious geniuses.

Adding to Torah in Every Generation

Traditional Judaism taught that religious inspiration of the highest level ended after the destruction of the First Temple. In some ways, Reform Jews agree with that. For Reform Jews, as for traditionalists, no book composed after the Bible has ever equaled that greatest of all works. For all that Jews respect the Talmud and Midrash, they are not as holy to us as is the Bible. The sort of geniuses the Jewish people had in the earliest centuries has never reappeared.

However, it would be a totally false impression of Judaism to believe that nothing religiously significant has happened during the nearly two thousand years since the Bible was completed. Quite the opposite is true. The Rabbis who created the Mishnah and Talmud devised and shaped the Jewish way of life. Most of our favorite celebrations—the Passover *seder, erev shabbat* candle lighting, *kiddush* and festive dinner, the wedding ceremony—were invented by them. They gave us the detailed laws which make justice and personal honesty so much a part of the way Jews are supposed to live. And they created the educational system that is still so important to Jews (although Jews now often turn their concern for a good education to university rather than *yeshivah* studies).

In the Middle Ages, European Jews created a rich spiritual life of their own despite the fact that they were continually oppressed by their non-Jewish neighbors. Reproductions of old illuminated manuscripts show us how medieval Jews mixed what they found acceptable in their Moslem and Christian surroundings with their sacred yet constantly changing Jewish heritage.

With so many American Jews descended from East European families, we are particularly conscious of the many contributions to a deeply Jewish kind of life that the immigrant families brought here with them. The Yiddish language is one example. It is full of Hebrew words and biblical expressions. Yiddish proverbs and jokes teach the old Torah lessons in ways that suit the experiences and needs of the joke tellers and their audiences.

Once the definition of "Torah" is no longer limited to the "words" God spoke to our ancestors, we can appreciate not only the great philosophers and scholars but all those other people who have felt God in their lives and found a way to express it.

This dynamic view of Torah was particularly important to the early Reform Jews. They were changing traditions that no longer seemed useful, yet were trying at the same time to remain faithful to Judaism. The Western ideas of order and beauty that they brought into services seemed strange and "unJewish" to people accustomed to another style. But their innovations should not be called unJewish. In fact, as time went on, the successful experiments at modernizing Judaism have themselves become part of the Torah tradition (and show the genius of their creators).

Continuing the Growth of Torah Today

Many very talented people today create songs, paintings, prayers, ceremonies, and books that give fresh insights into Judaism and help people become newly sensitive to God. Some of our most brilliant modern Jewish achievements come in areas that seem at first glance very far from Torah. Jewish summer camps that give modern American Jewish young people a chance to "live" Judaism fall into that category. So does the *oneg shabbat* after services, when the congregation gets a chance to spend time together in a relaxed way. "At the *oneg*," people share ideas and experiences and enjoy the feeling of being an extended, caring Jewish "family." The vast network of charitable activities that modern Jews have created and the remarkable number and variety of volunteer activities through which we support them are also part of the brilliant ways modern Jews make Torah live in our day.

We remain the people of Israel, trying to serve God today as best we can. As continuers of a four thousand year spiritual quest, we have to know the Torah tradition. At the same time, it must make sense to us. Therefore we create our own way in the present as other Jews did in the past. Our ances-

When we find ways to make Judaism—and Jewish values—central to our lives, we are creating Torah for our time.

A relief carved into these ark doors of white Appalachian oak shows Moses and Bezalel, the artisan who supervised construction of the Hebrews' desert sanctuary.

tors were the pioneers who marked the trail and showed us the path to take. We carry on the tradition of Torah they established, and add our insights to it as we prepare the way for other generations to come along and make the Torah their own.

One God

When our ancestors were exiled from the Land of Israel they had to clarify one aspect of their belief in God. Most ancient peoples believed that gods had power only in the territory where they were usually worshiped. If you left their land, you left them. New lands meant new gods. The Israelites could not believe their God was so limited. They realized their God must be everywhere. They said that God is one, the same, everywhere. The universe has but one God.

For modern Jews, the problem was not whether God was one or many, but whether the Jewish God was the one single God for all people. This was a question Jews had never needed to worry about before. In ancient Israel, Jews were the only monotheists (believers in one God). Later, there was so little contact between Jews and the monotheisms of Christianity and Islam that it didn't affect their lives. After Jews were forced into isolation in the ghettos, the nature of Christian belief wasn't of great interest to them.

However, when Jews began taking part in the modern world, they found a new way of thinking about God's "oneness." Jewish monotheism fit in spectacularly well with the new discoveries being made by scientists. Astronomy showed that there was an order in the universe. Evolution seemed to prove that there was a single pattern in nature. Einstein demonstrated that matter and energy are actually one. The more science showed that there really is order, the more reasonable it seemed that there is an "orderer"—One behind the many. Looked at that way, science lent support to the idea that there is one God over all.

Before the Emancipation, when Jews didn't have much opportunity to live freely among people who weren't Jewish, Judaism's ethical ideas were directed to other Jews. When Reform Jews became part of modern society, they saw that these Jewish teachings would also work very well for their new situation. If there is one God for all people, then everyone should be judged by the same standards—and no one need ever suffer discrimination. One God now meant one humankind, a powerful spur to living ethically.

This monotheistic emphasis helped the early Reformers see why they should stay Jews rather than become Christians. The Christian concept of the Trinity (the one God as Father, Son, and Holy Spirit) contradicted the Jewish understanding of God's unity. Even more significant for the Reformers, the Christians emphasized faith as the heart of their religion. Reform Jews felt that the most important part of being a religious person is doing good deeds—acting on one's beliefs. So they proudly described their religion as ethical monotheism.

New Ways of Thinking About God

We cannot explain the many modern Jewish ways of looking at God because our main concern here is Reform Judaism. Yet, it would give an incomplete picture of the Reform Jewish contributions to Judaism if we ignored modern religious ideas altogether. With the understanding that other courses will be necessary to cover the subject satisfactorily, let's take a very quick look at some of the ways Jews think about God today.

Most modern Jewish thinkers talk about God in terms of either ideas or feelings. Each of us reacts at times with our minds and, at other times, with our emotions. At a particular stage of life we may find one kind of explanation more satisfying than another—and then we may change our mind.

The concept of God as the one who orders science belongs in the category of ideas about God. If there is a unity that underlies science, and if things seemingly different from each other all turn out to be composed of energy, and if nature follows certain "laws," then that unity is what religion calls God.

Another idea comes from what science has learned about human behavior. According to social science, religion helps people live up to the best that is in them and in their groups. Religion does this by showing them that nature is on their side. Feeling that nature works for them, people place their trust in life and do the best they can in this world based on that trust. Religions give this sense of the helpfulness of the universe a name—they call it God, or gods. Some Jewish thinkers suggest that when we use the word God today, we should be implying all those forces in the universe that help us grow properly.

Some philosophers think of God as the most important "idea" of all, or as our human way of giving a name to everything that is good in the world. There are many other such approaches. If thinking of God as an "idea" appeals to you, you might want to find out more about these various philosophies.

The other way of thinking about God is through feelings. For some, this involves "sensing" that there are some things we will never be able to understand, no matter how advanced human scientific knowledge becomes. They believe that God is the "mystery" at the "heart" of life. Many people think that when human beings feel real love, involving all their emotions, they are experiencing God.

PART FOUR

What is a Reform Jew Supposed to Do?

If Reform Judaism insists that every individual Jew ought to be free to decide how he or she should live as a Jew, what makes them Jewish? What standards should Reform Jews use in making up their minds about how they will act? Are some parts of Judaism non-negotiable, or is everything subject to complete freedom of choice? What happens to the dissenters when most members of the Reform movement agree to take a united stand on a particular issue? Do Reform Jews have obligations outside the Reform movement? Beyond the Jewish community?

In this section of the book we will try to understand what a Reform Jew is supposed to do, and how Reform Jews ought to live their lives.

CHAPTER THIRTEEN

The Reform Jewish Emphasis on Ethics

W hat would you do if you were shopping with a group of friends and one of them took something from a store without paying for it? Would you be shocked? Or think it exciting? What if your friends began daring each other to shoplift—and there was no way for you to escape the challenge? It isn't easy to resist the pressure of a group, particularly when the members of the group are your friends or people you want to have as friends. But shoplifting is stealing. How much do you value right action? Enough to try to stop others from doing a bad thing? Enough to leave them and be unpopular for the sake of being ethical?

From its start, Reform Judaism has always said that acting ethically is the most important human obligation. Prayer, rituals and study are certainly all important parts of being a good Jew, but doing the right thing is the most important part of all. That, said the Reformers, is what God "wants" most from us.

The Reformers got this idea from the prophets. "Do good, not evil" seemed to be the message of every prophet. The Reformers called their special emphasis on ethics "prophetic Judaism."

If we look at the story of Amos, the first "literary" prophet, we will see these ideas clearly.

A Lonely Voice

In the eighth century B.C.E., the Land of Israel was divided into two king-doms. Jereboam was the highly successful ruler of the northern Jewish king-dom, known as Israel. He led Israel to war against its neighbors. The war made some people in his kingdom very rich. They had summer houses and winter homes. They showed off their precious jewels and elegant ivory carv-ings. Like many people who have suddenly gotten rich, they used their power to take advantage of the poor instead of helping them. And there were many poor people in Israel.

One man couldn't stand what was going on. He was not a government official or religious leader. He wasn't even from the northern kingdom. He came from Judah, the southern kingdom, where he worked as a shepherd. Yet he was so angry at the way he heard that people were treating one another that he traveled to Bethel, Jereboam's special city, to tell the Israelites that they were defying God. This man's name was Amos.

Amos went right to the king's temple and stood where everyone could hear him. He wanted to get the people's attention and he wanted them to keep listening. He started by attacking the enemies of Israel, one by one. He accused the Edomites, the Ammonites, the Moabites, and others of brutality. They broke treaties, murdered, sent people into exile. God would destroy them, Amos promised, "for three transgressions, or for four" they had com-mitted.

Then, surprisingly, he denounced Judah. Its people ignored the Torah, he said. They didn't observe God's laws. "For three transgressions of Judah, for four" will God "send down fire upon Judah and it shall devour the for-tresses of Jerusalem." No one in Israel had any great love for Judah. His words probably gave them even greater pleasure if they recognized by his accent that he was criticizing his own kinsmen.

But then, when he had his audience paying attention and agreeing with him, Amos turned the same sort of judgment on his listeners, the people of the Kingdom of Israel. And now he went into great detail.

You have "sold" honest justice "for silver," Amos told his audience. You have cheated the poor even for something as cheap as a pair of sandals. You have "trampled the heads of the poor into the dust." And at the same time, you've pampered yourselves with feasting and drinking and extravagance. You were warned, he told them, yet you ignored all the hints. God has seen "how many are your crimes, and how countless your sins—you enemies of the righteous, you takers of bribes, you who always judge the poor guilty." Be-cause you did evil, evil will be your reward. "Hear this," you fat cats (Amos called them "cows of Bashan"), you who "defraud the poor, who rob the

This is the decorative opening of a German-Hebrew edition of the Book of Amos.

needy," you will become slaves, you will go into exile in a foreign country. God will punish you for your sins by letting your enemies conquer you. "The great house shall be smashed to bits, and the little house to splinters."

Amos hoped somehow to convince them that although they were in danger of destruction there was still time to change their ways. They could save themselves if they would "seek good and not evil." God would not execute the harsh punishment they deserved if they would only learn to "hate evil and love good, and establish justice," if they would only listen to the voice of conscience.

No Excuses, No Bribes

He wouldn't give them any easy outs, either. Did the people think that God would never punish them because they were God's "chosen people"? They were wrong. That didn't mean the Jews were exempt from God's standards of holiness. If anything, they needed to behave better than other peoples in order to stay on good terms with God.

Speaking for God, Amos rejected their excuse in one powerful statement: "Only you, of all the families of earth, have I known (so closely), and that is why I will surely punish you for all your sins" (3:2). (Since that time, Jews have known that chosenness means responsibility, not privilege.)

The Israelites had another excuse: They were doing what they should—they regularly brought all the required sacrifices. Amos could not bear such a false understanding of Judaism. No amount of religious belief or practice would save them so long as they continued to act unethically. He wanted them to understand that God cares more about decency than about rituals.

So Amos the shepherd mocked their sacrifices and the way they bragged about how much they were giving. They announced their offerings as if they were bribing God to ignore the terrible injustice they were doing! "For you love that sort of thing, O Israelites." Amos let them know that God saw what hypocrites they were. He spoke in God's name:

> I loathe, I spurn your festivals,
> I am not appeased by your solemn assemblies.
> If you offer Me burnt offerings—or your meal offerings—
> I will not accept them;
> I will pay no heed
> to your gifts.
> Spare Me the sound of your hymns,
> And let Me not hear your lutes.

Fancy places to pray, elaborate rituals and long prayers are, by themselves, not what God wants. Being "religious" without doing good to other human beings is meaningless to God.

Amos had no doubt of what God "wants" most:

> Let justice well up like water,
> Righteousness like an unfailing stream.
>
> (5:21-24)

We are told a bit of what happened after Amos criticized the Israelites and prophesied what would become of them. Amaziah, priest at Bethel, complained about Amos to King Jereboam, accusing Amos of treason: "Our country cannot endure the things he is saying." He ordered Amos to get out of Israel immediately and go back to Judah. "Do your prophesying there. But don't ever prophesy again at Bethel, for it is a king's sanctuary and a royal palace."

Amos' response was simple (and inspiring to Jews ever after). He cared too much about justice to worry about his own safety, so he answered: "I am not a (professional) prophet, nor a prophet's son." I don't make my living

115

from doing this. I have spoken as I did because I had no choice but to speak out. "The Eternal One took me away from following the flock and said to me, 'Go, prophesy to My people Israel.' ".

> Does a lion roar in the forest
> When he has no prey? . . .
> A lion has roared,
> Who can but fear?
> My God, has spoken,
> Who can but prophesy?
> (3:4, 8)

Most of us do not have Amos' courage or even his certainty about what is right and what is wrong. But that is why our tradition cherishes his words and his message, and why we must try to learn from him and from the other prophets.

Prophetic Judaism: Reform's Choice

The prophetic teachings helped the early Reform Jews understand their responsibilities to the society which now welcomed them. Jews had lived in segregated Jewish communities for a long time. There was very little in their old books to guide them about Jewish responsibilities to a non-Jewish society. They had not been accepted as an equal part of one before the Emancipation so no one had tried to explain their duties.

Now the words of the prophets gave the Reformers the guidance they sought. The prophets said clearly that Israel was like the other nations, that the God of the Jewish people was the God of the entire universe. So if God's most important "demand" of Jews is that they treat people decently, then God must mean *all* people. Therefore, Jews have religious and ethical obligations to every human being and not just to other Jews. For the first time, Jewish teachers began saying that ethical duties to gentiles must be a major Jewish religious obligation. Even more, they insisted that trying to be good only to some people is unethical. We need to try to include everyone in our ethical concern. (This idea is called *universalism*. The opposite—concern for one group only—is called particularism.)

The prophets were not only talking about how individual people got along with one another, they were also concerned with society as a whole. They called for morality in politics, in war, in law, and in business. Their ethics are social ethics. They denounce cheating in business, exploiting the weak, defrauding the powerless, perverting justice for the sake of personal or national glory. They insist that no immoral society can survive for very long and they make the improvement of society a major Jewish concern.

116

The message of the prophets, urging us to act with ethical responsibility, is a crucial one to Reform Jews. This etching by Marc Chagall shows the prophet Jeremiah.

The Reformers were sure that the message of the prophets was much more important than the restrictions that separated Jews from the general society. Translated into specific terms this meant that keeping *kosher*, not riding on *Shabbat*, and other such laws mattered less to God than justice and righteous behavior. People could best be good Jews by being ethical human beings. If emancipated Jews were not bound by ritual restrictions, they could remain good Jews and at the same time participate fully in the civilization around them.

Then Why Stay Jewish?

This new connection of Judaism with universal ethics led to one problem. If Judaism is mainly ethics, why not give Judaism up altogether? Why not become decent Christians or a-religious citizens? Why bother with Judaism at all?

One part of the answer has to do with an important difference between Judaism and Christianity. Traditional Christians place more emphasis on "faith" than on "works." In other words, having the right belief—in Jesus—is the most important part of their religion. They believe that if you have the right faith you will then live decently. That is very different from the Jewish stress on *doing* the right thing. Judaism has always given detailed guidance as to what Jews should do. The Bible and the Talmud are full of commandments and religious statements about the right way to act. Jewish parents have been very concerned with what their children do, and the Jewish community celebrates Jewish virtues and criticizes Jewish wrongdoing. To give up Judaism for a faith without such strong ethical passion would be a great loss.

We also need Judaism because democracy itself does not create ethical behavior, nor does education alone make people moral. As recent American history has shown, being smart doesn't make a person good and being free doesn't make a person responsible. Conscience doesn't function automatically. It has to be properly developed through education and practice, and it has to be strengthened all the time. People do not behave decently unless they believe that justice and mercy are the most important values in life—regardless of what the majority thinks or does. Many people in society today act as if they do not care at all about ethical behavior. But it will always be the essence of Reform Judaism.

CHAPTER FOURTEEN

Reform Jewish Duties: Ethics Plus

Some Jews say, "If the Orthodox have the most things to do, the Conservatives less, and Reform Jews the least, then the Orthodox are the most Jewish, Conservative Jews less, and Reform Jews the least Jewish." That mistakenly identifies being a good Jew with practicing a traditional list of observances, like keeping kosher, wearing a *kippah* all the time, or not riding on Shabbat. Reform Jews have a different idea of what a good Jew ought to do and we want to explain it.

Remember: No one is going to tell you what you *must* do. Reform Judaism believes that caring, educated individuals have the right to make up their own minds about their Jewish duties. The first step is to prepare properly for our choices.

That begins with knowing something about our tradition. For thousands of years Jews have thought about how to live a good Jewish life. Most Reform Jews find, when they read old Jewish texts, that we're not very different from Jews in other times and places. So they can help us be responsible Jews. As they were trying to serve God, so should we. Often no rule can help us. We need to rely on our sense of God. In such a situation we need to ask what we most deeply believe God "wants" us to do. Judaism teaches that each of us, in our own way, can reach out to God. If we make such reaching out a regular part of our life, when we are faced with a difficult problem our sense of closeness to God can be a great help in finding the right solution.

The Kind of Duties with Which We Should be Concerned

A number of years ago the Reform rabbis' organization listed their understanding of every Jew's obligations in nine categories:

1. Ethical Obligations

Our first duty is to be just and decent to every human being—in our own family, in school, in the community, in business and wherever else we have dealings with people. In everything we do, all our lives, we must strive to do what is right. Sometimes, when we hear reports of unfairness and cruelty, we are tempted to say "that's someone else's business" and do nothing. Judaism teaches us that it is our obligation to reach beyond ourselves to help improve the world to the best of our ability. That is why Jews have been—and

A Jewish wedding sanctifies the establishment of a Jewish home, centered on family devotion.

Lifelong study.

must continue to be—involved in individual acts and movements to safeguard human rights and protect the freedom of every single person.

2. A Jewish Home Centered on Family Devotion

The closeness of family ties and family loyalty have been among the most appealing features of Judaism throughout our history. Jewish law requires parents to educate their children, and demands that children respect their parents. These obligations form the basis for a lifetime of mutual caring and love. The Jewish home has traditionally been a place where members of the family can find reassurance and reinforcement—whatever may be happening in the world outside.

3. Lifelong Study

The teachings of Judaism are designed to help us understand our relationship with God and to guide us in living our lives. If you stop studying about Judaism when you are confirmed, you will have only a child's view of Judaism. People who do not continue learning about Judaism after they become adults cannot possibly live their lives intelligently according to Jewish principles, or defend Judaism against clever detractors.

4. Private Prayer and Public Worship

We Jews pray as a community, reciting together the ideals we believe in, renewing regularly our relationship with God, joining with other Jews to gain the strength that comes from feeling part of a group. Judaism also teaches the importance of praying alone, at any time or place. Prayers of thanks to God for good things that happen to us, and expressions of our hopes and fears are the appropriate and natural outpourings of our souls. Often there are things that trouble or move us very deeply. No one else knows what is on our minds so only we, personally, can express it properly—whether we say the words out loud or pray silently. But even without a crisis, we should learn to stop now and then to renew our own personal sensitivity to God, the most important reality in the universe.

5. Daily Religious Observance

Judaism cannot be limited to Friday night or Saturday morning. We should be living our religion every day. There are special blessings for waking up each morning, on seeing a rainbow, taking a trip, eating the first fruits of the season, surviving a dangerous event. Just as God "renews the work of creation every day"—the sun rises, the grass grows, new babies are born—so should we renew our sense of appreciation and gratitude. And when it is time for sleep, we can be thankful for today and hopeful for every tomorrow.

6. Keeping Shabbat and Holy Days

Observing Shabbat and Jewish festivals testifies to our faith in God and our ties to the religious history of our people. These celebrations can strengthen the feelings of closeness within our families and our concern for one another in the Jewish community. Shabbat and festival observances unite God, Torah and the Jewish people through unique, immediate experiences.

7. Celebrating Life Cycle Events

Certain occasions in life are very special—the birth of a child, Bar and Bat Mitzvah, Confirmation, marriage and death. These are times when we look at who we are, where we have come from, and what our future might hold. The answers to all these questions are inseparable from our belief in God. Therefore, Jews mark each of these life cycle events with the religious ceremonies of our people.

8. Involvement with the Synagogue and the Community

The synagogue has traditionally served as much more than only a place for worship and study. People get together in the synagogue to socialize, to share ideas, concerns, sorrows and joys. In this sense, the synagogue is both an extended Jewish family and a miniature Jewish community. Every Jew ought to be involved in his/her own congregation. But we are also a part of the larger Jewish community: national and international. We need to join in building the great cultural and educational institutions that express the creative energies of our people. And we need to reach out personally with caring and friendship to all Jews, near and far, those like us and those very different from us. We need to meet the needs of the poor, the troubled, the oppressed and those whose lives are in danger.

Activities that help the Jewish people survive.

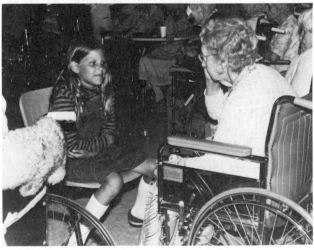

9. Activities that Help the Jewish People Survive and Better the Life of Jews Everywhere

Among the most important tasks of the Jewish community are defending and protecting the rights of Jews around the world. Even after the Holocaust and the creation of the State of Israel, we find it necessary to struggle for Jews in the former Soviet Union, in Arab lands, in South America, in Africa—and in our own country and in the Jewish homeland itself. Without Jews, there is no Judaism. And we have an obligation to help Jews build and maintain a vigorous religious and cultural life, in the many ways this is possible, all over the world.

Dealing with the Obligations

What is your reaction to these nine categories? Do you think that you need all of these areas in order to lead a good Jewish life? Different people will have different opinions about the order and importance of these areas of Jewish duty. From a Reform point of view, that is a good thing. Variety which comes out of knowledge and belief is precious to Reform Judaism. As long as people are serious about their religion, everyone can learn and grow by listening to other people's ideas.

But that means that the Reform standard of what makes a good Jew isn't a list of rules. The *way* people decide things is much more important than whether or not they agree with us—or with each other—on the specifics of what they choose to do or not do. If they are committed to the Jewish people and a relationship with God and make responsible decisions in terms of their commitment, we consider them "good Jews."

Now look at the items below. A number of these are traditional Jewish duties. Others are modern adaptations. Use them to see what specific things you think ought to be part of your way of living as a Jew. Try to decide in which of the nine categories of Reform Jewish duty they belong.

Bar/Bat Mitzvah
love
thanking God
hunger relief
chopping *haroset*
Jewish Chautauqua Society
Talmud
United Jewish Appeal
a day of complete rest
singing with the congregation
social action
keeping kosher
Hebrew
being grateful you've gotten better after being sick
respecting parents
Confirmation
circumcision *(brit milah)*
Joint Distribution Committee
Legal Aid Society
special family outings
funeral service
world peace

marching in the Israel Day parade
absorbing Russian immigrants
learning the lessons of the Holocaust
wearing *tefillin*
wedding ceremony
noticing the beauty of nature
raising children
modern Jewish philosophy
attending services
Sisterhood, Brotherhood, Youth Group
sticking up for your brother/sister
United Way
making blessings before each meal *(motzi)*
hearing the shofar blown
Union of American Hebrew Congregations
adult Torah study class
Anti-Defamation League

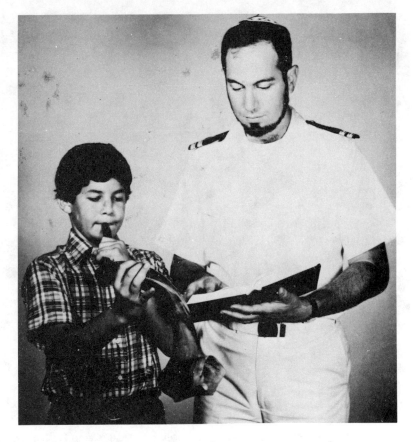

It is a mitzvah to hear the shofar. A Jewish chaplain in the United States Navy is assisted by one of his young congregants.

Too many Reform Jews, we are sorry to say, are much more expert at choosing what they *won't* do than what they will. So we want to try one more exercise to show how Jewish tradition can help us make intelligent decisions about how we should live. Look at the list below. Most are traditional quotations. Some come from the Bible, many from the Talmud. Which lead you to a more positive sense of your Jewish obligations? Which do not? Even if you can't make up your mind, this should illustrate how Jewish study can help guide you—and we hope it is a process you will be going through all your life.

"Where is God? Wherever you let God in" (R. Mendel of Kotzk).

"*Tzedakah* knows neither race nor creed" (Gittin 61a).

"The Sabbath was given to you—you were not given to the Sabbath" (Yoma 85b).

"To love God truly, one must first love people. And if anyone tells you about loving God but not loving other people, you will know that person is lying" (based on Martin Buber).

In the "chapel in the woods," a counselor at UAHC Camp Harlam becomes a Bat Mitzvah.

"Every day will I bless You, and I will praise Your Name for ever and ever" (Psalm 145:2).

"All Israel is responsible for one another" (Sifra 112a to Lev. 26:34).

"O God, You are near to all who call upon You, to all who call upon You in truth" (Psalm 145:18).

"When our learning is greater than our deeds we are like trees with many branches and only a few roots: the wind comes and uproots them. ... But when our deeds are greater than our learning we are like trees with only a few branches but with many roots, so that even if all the winds of the world were to come and blow against them, they would be unable to topple the tree" (Pirke Avot 3:22).

"God creates new worlds constantly—by causing marriages to take place" (Zohar).

"When one does *tzedakah* and justice, it is as if the whole world is filled with kindness" (Sukkah 49b).

"Seek peace and pursue it" (Psalm 34:15).

"As this child has entered into the Covenant of Abraham, so may he enter into the study of Torah, the blessing of marriage, and the practice of goodness" (*brit milah* ceremony, *Gates of the House*).

"This is the day that God has made; let us rejoice and be glad on it" (Psalm 118:24).

"Unhappiness in a home is like rottenness in fruit" (Sotah 3b).

"Justice, justice shall you pursue" (Deut. 16:20).

"Have we not all one father? Has not one God created us? Why do we deal treacherously every man against his brother, profaning the covenant of our ancestors?" (Malachi 2:10).

"Get yourself a teacher; acquire a friend to study with you" (Avot 1:6).

"What was created on the Sabbath day? Contentment, peace of mind, and physical rest" (Genesis Rabbah 10:12).

"Do not separate yourself from the community" (Avot 2:5).

"Prayer without the heart is like a body without spirit" (Bahya Ibn Pakuda).

"It has been told you, O mortal, what is good, and what the Eternal One requires of you: Only to do justice, and to love mercy, and to walk humbly with your God" (Micah 6:8).

"In a place where no one behaves like a human being, you must strive to be human" (Avot 2:6).

"The honor due to parents is like the honor due to God" (Mekhilta to Ex. 20:12).

"Eternal God, Creator of day and night . . . bless my family and friends, all those I love, all who love me. May my dreams be pleasant ones, and may I wake up with a smile, ready for the new day" (Evening prayer, *Gates of the House*).

"Great is peace! Hateful is quarreling!" (Sifra to Parashat Naso 2).

"The prayer of one who prays with the community will be granted" (Berakhot 8a).

127

Members of a Reform youth group were reaching out to the community when they helped restore a dilapidated inner city synagogue.

"These are My fixed times, the fixed times of the Eternal One, which you shall proclaim as sacred occasions" (Lev. 23:2).

"As my ancestors planted (trees) for me, so do I plant for my children" (Ta'anit 23a).

"Blessed is the Eternal One our God, ruler of the universe, for giving us life, for sustaining us, and for enabling us to reach this day" (traditional prayer book).

"All are equal before God in prayer" (Exodus Rabbah 21:4).

"Do not say, 'when I have leisure I shall study'—you may never find the time" (Avot 2:5).

"A little hurt from a relative is worse than a big hurt from a stranger" (Zohar).

"I make pleasant songs, and weave verses, because my soul longs for You" (Judah of Regensburg).

"These are the obligations without measure, whose reward, too, is without measure: to honor father and mother; to perform acts of love and kindness; to attend the house of study daily; to welcome the stranger; to visit the sick; to rejoice with bride and groom; to console the bereaved; to pray with sincerity; to make peace where there is strife. And the study of Torah is equal to them all" (Peah 1:1), "because," *Gates of Prayer* adds, "it leads to them all."

Jewish teachings can be a great help to us in making decisions. But when complicated new problems arise, our tradition doesn't always have clear-cut answers easily available. Should I get a job or go on to college? Should I refuse to register for the draft? How do I feel about having my dying relative taken off life support systems? Should I do everything possible to make sure that person is kept alive? For how long?

In many situations, only we, personally, can make the final decision. Making choices and learning to live by them is hard work. That is why Reform Judaism is not for everyone. Fortunately, some Jews are willing to take their Judaism and their human freedom very seriously. They are the minority that keep Judaism alive. We hope that you will feel that way too, and choose to be part of the active minority who are the glory and hope of Reform Judaism.

CHAPTER FIFTEEN

How We Decide Just What We Need to Do

From time to time, congregations have to make certain choices. Your congregation had to decide whether or not to use the new prayer book, *Gates of Prayer*, when it came out. Did the concern for contemporary issues meet your congregation's needs? Did the modern English make too many members of your synagogue uncomfortable? Your congregation's board or membership debated the matter and then made a democratic decision. No outsider told them what their congregation *had* to do. They were free, as thoughtful Jews, to choose what they deemed best.

Similarly, the Reform movement as a whole often has to decide what official position to take on a complicated issue. How do Reform Jews feel, for instance, about encouraging the *aliyah* of American families to Israel? Should there be a Reform statement on abortion, or on child abuse? Should the Reform movement take a stand on environmental protection?

This kind of decision-making involves many people—representatives of the more than 850 congregations that make up the Union of American Hebrew Congregations plus the more than 1500 rabbis who belong to the Central Conference of American Rabbis. A majority must agree that the decision being made is right for Reform Jews. Yet even when a decision is reached it is only a guideline, not a binding rule. Individual congregations or rabbis or Jews are free to disagree. Once a large number of Reform congregations and Reform rabbis have made the decision part of their congregational life, it becomes part of mainstream Reform Judaism, like a positive attitude toward Zionism or concern with everyone's civil rights.

To see how this process works, let's look at three specific changes that were introduced into Reform Judaism. One has been generally accepted; one has been almost universally rejected; and the third is still being fought out.

Case One: The Equality of Women

The idea of equality for women seemed logical to the early Reformers, since they believed that everyone deserved equal opportunities. You remember that even in the earliest days of Reform, girls studied together with boys. They celebrated their Confirmation together. Women joined the formerly all-male synagogue choirs, then left the women's galleries and sat with the men at services.

As early as 1845, the German Reform rabbis agreed that "woman has the same obligation as man to participate from youth up in the public services and that the custom not to include woman in a (*minyan*) is only a custom and has no religious basis." A year later, the group said that there must be "complete religious equality of woman with man" and that women had "equal religious obligation." In the United States, in 1892, the CCAR—only a few years after it was started—voted Reform Jewish women eligible for "full membership with all the privileges of voting and holding office in our congregations."

Real equality came slowly, however. It was easier to announce equal rights than to put them into effect in a world ruled by men. (Consider how long it took after American women won the right to vote before women were elected to significant offices.) Since no records mention the first female delegate to a Union Biennial, it was obviously not considered an outstanding occasion worthy of self-congratulation.

Still, until the 1950s, congregational boards of trustees were almost universally male. As a result of the women's liberation movement in the 1960s, Reform Jewish women began to reexamine their role in Jewish life. They urged their congregations to put the theoretical beliefs about women's equality into actual practice.

At first it seemed strange to have women involved in aspects of synagogue life not connected to Sisterhood, the religious school, or the preparation and serving of food. Seeing women sit on the *bimah* or receive an *aliyah* to the Torah seemed wrong to many people. They weren't used to it

Before the Reform movement made women equal to men in religious life, women sat in a separate section when they came to synagogue.

Since 1972, the Reform movement has ordained women as rabbis. This photograph was taken at the ordination ceremony for the New York campus of HUC-JIR, held at Temple Emanuel.

and they weren't comfortable with it. It violated their idea of what was "right" in a service. Individual congregations struggled hard with these issues. As the years passed, virtually every Reform congregation decided that "not being used to something" is far less important than ethical fairness—and equality for women has increasingly won out.

It took many more years before women became rabbis. As long ago as 1922, the CCAR declared that "women cannot justly be denied the privilege of ordination." But not until 1967, when Sally Priesand applied to the college for admission, was a woman accepted into the rabbinical school for the purpose of being ordained. In 1972, the Hebrew Union College-Jewish Institute of Religion became the first Jewish seminary to ordain a woman as rabbi. Many women have since become rabbis and cantors. Although they have won much respect, they still face special problems.

Reform Jews have taken other stands opposing discrimination against women. UAHC Biennial resolutions have supported women's rights, passage of the Equal Rights Amendment to the United States Constitution, and legislation on issues like battered women.

The prayer book most Reform congregations use today, *Gates of Prayer*, only partially has overcome the masculine bias of traditional Judaism. Often it talks about our "ancestors," but occasionally it still says "our fathers." Although some texts say "he," others say "a person" or "one." We still have a lot to learn about how we can write prayers or refer to God in non-sexist ways. But we are moving steadily to make our ethics more effective in our lives.

Most Reform Jews are now comfortable with the fuller role women play in Reform Jewish life. It seems impossible to many Reform Jews that equality will not someday be extended to women in every movement in Judaism.

On the whole, the case of women's rights is a good example of how the Reform movement has agreed on an important decision despite considerable problems along the way.

Case Two: The Disappearance of the Sunday Service

Sometimes, what seems to help keep Judaism alive in one generation is rejected by a later one. About a hundred years ago, American Reform Jews had a serious problem. Although Jewish law said that the Friday service welcoming Shabbat must be held at sunset, most men couldn't leave their jobs early enough to get to synagogue in time for the service. (Traditionally, women rarely if ever attended that service because they were busy at home preparing Shabbat dinner.)

In addition, Saturday morning was no longer a "logical" time for services. The majority of people had to work on Saturday morning. If everyone else in America was working, refusing to do so would be asking for trouble.

The Sabbath seemed in danger of dying. Most Reform Jews—actually, most American Jews, whatever their denomination—didn't attend either sundown services on Friday or the Saturday morning service. The leaders of the Reform movement realized that something had to be done to save Jewish public prayer.

Reform rabbis in Germany had already come up with one idea: Since no one worked on Sunday mornings, why not switch the major service-going day from Saturday to Sunday? There was no need to call Sunday "Shabbat." They would simply use the prayer book's service for weekdays. So American Reform temples also began experimenting with a Sunday morning service. At the beginning of the twentieth century, as many as fifty Reform congregations around the country (a large proportion of the then small movement) were holding their major service on Sunday morning. For some people it was a satisfying solution.

Other Reform Jews were troubled. Sunday services just didn't seem "Jewish" enough even if they brought many Jews into the synagogue. These Jews believed Shabbat was too central to Jewish tradition to get traded off for such small gains.

In 1902, the CCAR appointed a special committee to examine this Shabbat question. For the following ten years the subject was debated at each annual conference. No vote was taken and no absolute policy established. Rabbi Jacob Voorsanger argued that Sunday services destroyed "the solidarity and identity" of the Jewish people, that the Sabbath is a "historical institution" that "represents principles that are part of the life blood of our religion." If we break the "chain of centuries" it will be our loss, because it "will separate us from our people all over the world."

But Rabbi Hyman G. Enelow said that the "spiritual ideas" of Judaism were always more important than the way that ceremonies were observed. Therefore, he insisted, "the religious end of the Sabbath may be reached on another day. . . . We want to save the Sabbath for Judaism. . . . Even if the Sabbath were to serve above all as a symbol of Israel's unity, I should feel more closely related to a number of Jews observing a true Sabbath any day of the week than to such as cling to the Saturday Sabbath in no way save by word of mouth."

Rabbi Isaac Mayer Wise and a few of his colleagues had already found an alternative as early as 1869. Wise reported their suggestion in his magazine, *The American Israelite*. Their idea, too, went against traditional Jewish law. But they felt that—in contrast to the Sunday service—their suggestion did not violate the spirit of Jewish belief. Their radical change was to not start the Friday evening service at sunset but to wait until well into the evening. This

Some Reform congregations experimented with holding their major service on Sunday morning. A much more successful experiment, and one practiced by most congregations today, was the introduction of a late Friday evening service.

"My House shall be called a House of Prayer for All Peoples"

Temple Berith Kodesh
ROCHESTER · NEW YORK

SUNDAY SERVICE

permitted people to finish work, go home and clean up, eat Shabbat dinner with their families, and then attend synagogue together. It also allowed women to join their husbands for services. The entire family could now pray together on the day Jews had traditionally set aside for worship.

Over the years, most Reform Jews came to consider the Sunday service a bad idea. Wise's idea provided a much better solution to the problem because it answered the need in a "more" Jewish way. Hardly any congregations have Sunday services today.

The late Friday evening service has become so much a part of American Jewish life that almost all Conservative and some Orthodox congregations have a Shabbat service at that time. Many American Jews today probably don't realize that the late Friday evening service is a Reform innovation hardly more than one hundred years old, nor do they know about the unsuccessful Sunday morning experiment.

Case Three: Should Reform Rabbis Perform Intermarriages?

We now turn to a topic where very big differences of opinion still exist, so let's make certain that we all understand the terms we are using. *Intermarriage* means a marriage between a Jew and someone who is not Jewish. (This is also sometimes called a mixed marriage, referring to the *mix* of two religions.) When one of the partners to a marriage officially leaves his/her religion and accepts the religion of the other partner (or at any time a person takes the necessary steps to change religions), that person is a *convert* and the process is known as *conversion*. Once someone has converted to Judaism, the person is a Jew—and a marriage between a convert and a born Jew is *not* an intermarriage. Some Jews mistakenly think that a person who has converted to Judaism is less Jewish than a born Jew, or even a kind of "second class" Jew. There is no basis in Jewish tradition or modern Judaism for that judgment. Most "Jews by choice" have studied about Jewish history and obligations and are therefore more knowledgeable and more enthusiastic about being good Jews than the majority of Jews who know little, care little, and do little.

The problem we want to look at here is not conversion or even whether or not to accept intermarried couples as members of Reform congregations. Most synagogues have no difficulty welcoming intermarried couples into congregational life. The unresolved question involves what Reform rabbis ought to be doing. Specifically, should Reform rabbis perform intermarriages?

Obviously, Reform rabbis have the "right" to do whatever they want. Legally, they are licensed to perform whatever marriages they wish by the states in which they function. Religiously, the Reform movement has no laws binding rabbis or the power to forbid their doing something—or any interest in doing so.

But as a matter of personal religious decision, is it proper for a rabbi to perform a wedding ceremony for someone who isn't Jewish? Doesn't it seem to be giving approval to intermarriage at a time when the Jewish community is worried about the lack of Jewish commitment in Jewish families?

The rabbis who perform intermarriages say that what they are doing will help the Jewish community. They quote statistics showing that the majority of intermarried couples choose the Jewish community when they choose to be involved in a religion, and that they raise their children as Jews. These rabbis point out that many non-Jewish partners even convert to Judaism later on. They believe that by welcoming the newly married couple and making them feel that they can find a home within Judaism the rabbi is helping keep them as part of the Jewish community. They say that rabbis who refuse to perform

On the _____ day of the week, the _____ day of the month in the year five thousand seven hundred _____ corresponding to the secular date, _____, in the city of _____ there came before us, the undersigned witnesses, the Groom _____ and the Bride _____

The groom made the following declaration: "Be sanctified to me as my wife according to the traditions of Moses and Israel, and I will love, honor and respect you. I will provide for you and sustain you as is proper for a Jewish husband to do for his wife." And the bride accepted his words.

The bride made the following declaration: "Be sanctified to me as my husband according to the traditions of Moses and Israel, and I will love, honor and respect you. I will provide for you and sustain you as is proper for a Jewish wife to do for her husband." And the groom accepted her words.

The bride and groom hereby enter into the sacred covenant of marriage -Kiddushin-and agree to establish a Jewish home together according to the traditions of our people.
In expression of their acceptance of this Ketubah the groom _____ and the bride _____ have affixed their signatures to this document in the presence of the witnesses undersigned in accordance with the traditions of Judaism,

and everything herein is valid and proper.

Bride _____   Groom _____
Witness _____   Witness _____
_____ Rabbi

May there be peace in their home, confidence and serenity in their hearts

(Above) This is the English part of the Reform movement's *ketubah,* the Jewish marriage contract.

(Left) Standing under the *huppah,* a bride and groom drink from the same cup in symbolic recognition of their pledge to share whatever life will bring.

mixed marriages are discouraging Jewish families and chasing away future Jews.

Needless to say, the Reform rabbis who do not perform intermarriages disagree. They feel that they have been ordained to serve the Jewish community and that their authority extends only to Jews. They believe that when they perform a wedding ceremony they are giving the marriage the blessing of God and the Jewish people. It seems to them that sanctifying an intermarriage makes a mockery of the values of Judaism. These rabbis—and they are the majority of the Reform rabbinate—don't agree that sanctioning an intermarriage significantly increases the Jewish community. They are suspicious of these statistics and cite statistics that are far more negative. They feel they can appropriately welcome an intermarried couple into the community without lending their presence to an event of which they do not approve. Besides, they find it nonsensical to urge kids not to interdate or to encourage them to marry only Jews, if they then reward those who go against the community ideal with the full blessings of Judaism.

Two important Reform Jewish values clash here. The emphasis on ethics and the equality of all people would seem to make marrying any good person a reasonable thing to do. And perhaps intermarriage wouldn't matter so much if there were hundreds of millions of Jews in the world and we weren't so strongly convinced that Judaism must be preserved. But the survival of the Jewish people and the perpetuation of Judaism are critical to us. The world Jewish population is very small, so every Jewish family matters very much for keeping Judaism alive.

There is another reason why many Reform rabbis feel that it is not right for them to perform intermarriages. They are concerned about the rest of the Jewish people. They want to get along with Conservative and Orthodox Jews for the sake of community causes at home and to help strengthen the Reform movement in Israel. They believe that if Reform rabbis cooperate with the other movements in areas concerning who is a Jew and perform marriage and conversion ceremonies according to traditional law the others will have less reason to oppose Reform.

After some years of passionate debate, the CCAR passed a resolution in 1973 urging Reform rabbis not to perform intermarriages. The new resolution only reaffirmed what had already been said as early as 1909 (the problem extends back at least that far). Individual rabbis of course continued to have the right to follow their own consciences if they disagreed with the decision, as many did.

In spite of that, many people were afraid then that the decision would rip the Reform movement apart. The problem was not simply one of performing intermarriages. Some rabbis believed that when the Reform movement told rabbis that they should not do intermarriages it was, in effect, trying to take away their freedom to choose for themselves. Other rabbis argued that in such serious matters there had to be limits on personal autonomy. They said that Jews who misused their freedom to the point of destroying the most sacred remaining practices of our people were no longer acting as Jews. In a way, this sounds very much like the arguments over Sunday services in the first decade of this century. Once again, the need to adapt and the need to remain Jewish are in conflict.

Though the argument still goes on, two important things have emerged. First, even though most Reform rabbis disagree with the pro-intermarriage position of the minority, the majority understands that those who perform intermarriages do so because they believe that they are acting in the best interests of Judaism.

Second, the rabbis learned once again—and went back and shared the message with their congregations—that the Reform movement must be prepared to live even with bitter differences of opinion in order to survive creatively, to grow, and to serve the changing needs of Reform Jews.

As you can see in this case, there is no generally accepted Reform Jewish decision. What has been agreed upon is a way of slowly trying to reach one.

Making responsible decisions is hard for individuals and perhaps even harder for groups—whether the group is your congregation or the Reform movement as a whole. Is being a Reform Jew and caring very much about responsible use of freedom worth the work? We think so.

CHAPTER SIXTEEN

Our Relation to the State of Israel

Do you know someone who wasn't very enthusiastic about going on a trip to Israel? Was that person dragged along or sent by parents, or grudgingly gave in to the husband's or wife's eagerness to visit? What a change takes place when the trip is over! Most people have a very special response to Israel. Even Jews who didn't think they cared find that their feelings about the country and the people are far deeper and stronger than they had imagined.

If you are lucky enough to have gone to Israel already, or are planning to go after Confirmation (with your Confirmation class or with groups like NFTY), you will be able to experience this for yourself.

Why do we Jews have such powerful feelings about Israel?

Our Bible and prayer books talk about the Land of Israel and the people of Israel all the time. The Haggadah ends with the wish, "next year in Jerusalem." Traditionally, Jews pray facing east, toward Jerusalem. Israel, as land and as people, has been one of the central ideas of Judaism. During the nearly two thousand years when most Jews lived outside the Land of Israel, it continued to be the focus of their hopes and dreams. It was the symbol of Jewish freedom, the opposite of persecution, the ideal goal.

Israel is much more than a symbol today, much more than an idea—or an ideal. It is a real place. Names like Jerusalem, the Jordan River, the Golan Heights, Tel Aviv, the Dead Sea and the Negev are so familiar to us that we sometimes forget that there hasn't always been a modern State of Israel. For almost two thousand years Jews had no country of their own—no place where they made the laws or provided for their own safety. In 1948, after the most horrible suffering in Jewish history, a modern sort of miracle took place: the State of Israel was established.

Creating a New Way of Living

In Israel, street signs, billboards, and TV commercials are all in Hebrew. Babies talk Hebrew. Dogs and cats respond to Hebrew commands. Yet classical Hebrew obviously did not have a word for electricity, or elevator, or jet plane, or nuclear capability, or even ice cream cone or sweater. Hebrew had to be turned into a modern language.

When you visit Israel for the first time, it is a surprise to discover that almost everyone is Jewish. The garbage collectors are Jews. The telephone operators are Jews. The heads of government are Jews. Jewish policemen chase Jewish criminals and haul them into Jewish courts where Jewish lawyers plead their cases before Jewish judges. It isn't easy to remember that most of these people are Jews. For one thing, we aren't used to the idea of a Jewish majority. For another, many of them don't "look" Jewish to our American eyes. They look like Arabs or Russians or Indians. They have come to Israel from all over the world.

Working Together to Build Israel

Despite the great cultural differences between Ashkenazi and Sephardi Jews, between observant and non-observant Jews, between Jews from technologically sophisticated Western nations and those from Oriental countries, they have done remarkable things together. A hundred years ago the land was comparatively empty of people. In many places it was barren, treeless, and swampy. Robber bands roamed unchecked.

Brave Jewish immigrants drained the dangerous swamps, defended their settlements, wiped out disease and introduced modern agriculture and industry. They made Israel a beautiful, fertile country with thriving cities, towns, and agricultural settlements. One of the most dramatic things that you see when you travel in Israel is the difference between the barren, rocky hills and the green ones from which the stones have been removed and crops or trees

Two residents of Ramat Hashikmah, an Israeli neighborhood helped by Project Renewal, enjoy a few quiet moments in the late afternoon sun.

planted in their place. Backbreakingly hard work and years of devotion have made the difference. The Israelis have planted more than one hundred and thirty million trees so far, possibly the largest environmental renewal project in history. You have probably shared in this work too, by "planting" your own trees through the Jewish National Fund.

Today, the Israelis are desalinating sea water, farming by an ingenious system of computerized "drip irrigation" and inventing other effective ways to maximize the use of water. They have already begun teaching other nations about water conservation (something that will become ever more desperately necessary as the years go by). They are among the leading experimenters with solar energy and medical technology. Israel produces a majority of all the lasers used for surgery around the world, to give only one technological example. The list of their special accomplishments could go on and on. And all of these inventions and developments—even the military ones—have human life and safety as their primary concern.

The Democracy in the Middle East

The Arab countries opposed the creation of the State of Israel in 1948 and have threatened Israel's security ever since. One of the first things Jews who settle in Israel have had to learn is how to defend themselves. They have learned well. Israel's Defense Forces are among the best in the world.

Israel is a fully democratic country, unlike most of the other countries founded since World War II. Most of the others are dictatorships, usually run by the military—including the ones that claimed they were democracies when they started out. Israel has very distinct political parties and free, vigorous debates on all public issues. Despite the ever-present danger of war and terrorism, Israelis have a deep concern for individual human lives, for freedom of expression, and for the quality of life in their country.

Publishing houses in Israel today provide books of poetry, plays, novels, and scholarly works to a Hebrew-speaking public eager to read them. Israel publishes more books *per capita* every year than any other country. An incredible number of newspapers in a variety of languages are on the newsstands every day. Israel has theater companies, dance troupes, and orchestras

It took massive drainage projects to rid Israel of malaria-infested swamps. Today this land is among the most fertile parts of the country.

"If you will it," wrote Theodor Herzl, "it is no dream." With similar energy and courage, the young Israelis of today dream about the accomplishments of tomorrow.

that perform all over the world. You may have a painting or sculpture by an Israeli artist in your home or in your synagogue or Jewish community center.

The seven Israeli universities are world famous in many secular fields and set the standard for Jewish scholarship everywhere.

These human and cultural accomplishments are particularly impressive when we think about what most immigrants had to endure before reaching Israel. Refugees from the Holocaust—the survivors of the ghettos and concentration camps, their lives shattered by the Nazis—came to Israel. Jews came from Arab countries where many of them had lived in poverty and were treated with contempt by their Arab "masters." Some of these Oriental Jews were unprepared for freedom or even for twentieth century Western style commonplaces like public education, automobiles, or indoor plumbing. The most recent great wave of immigrants, Soviet Jews, carried with them bitter thoughts of the gulags of Siberia and the degradation of life as "refuseniks."

Many Jews arrived in Israel burdened with the horrors and frustrations of their past. Getting them to lead normal, healthy, and productive lives has been one of Israel's major goals. It has been a difficult job—and there are still many unsolved problems—but it is the kind of effort a Jewish state knows is critical. Israel's success as a nation is largely due to the way people from widely different backgrounds have learned to work together and contribute their varied skills for their country's good.

In spite of these wonderful achievements, Israel is constantly being criticized by other nations around the world. The United Nations, in a vicious political move that substituted propaganda for intelligence, called Zionism "racism." When the Jordanians destroyed portions of the Jewish cemetery on the Mount of Olives and used Jewish tombstones as building stones for sidewalks and latrines in Jordanian army camps, no international outcry was raised. Yet Israel, which carefully protects all of the Christian and Moslem holy places, is continually being accused in the United Nations of desecrating these sites.

The rest of the world could learn an inspiring message from Israel: People do not have to give in to defeat or hatred. It is possible, even in the midst of an insane world, to create a place where people are willing to behave decently, care about one another, and build a cultured civilization that gives human needs top priority.

Reform Judaism's Changing Relationship to Israel

Reform Jews have re-formed relationships to Israel. Way back when becoming accepted as citizens of their new country dominated the lives of Reform Jews, Zionism seemed like a conflicting goal. As we discussed before, many Reform Jews were anti-Zionist, although some Reform Jews were always among the key leaders of the Zionist movement.

Even before Hitler's rise to power, this attitude was changing. By 1942, the official position of the Reform movement, favoring the establishment of a Jewish State in Palestine, caused a small group of diehard anti-Zionists to break away from the movement. They founded the American Council for Judaism, which still exists and still fights every effort to connect American Jews with the State of Israel. The overwhelming majority of Reform Jews, however, has strongly supported the State of Israel since its establishment.

The unique opportunities Israel offers for being a Jew are clear. Nowhere else in the world do Jews have the Jewish opportunities that are theirs in Israel. In Israeli public schools, the Bible is taught as national history. Scout troops and youth groups take hikes to the place where Elijah had his contest with the priests of Baal, picnic on the spot where David hid from King Saul, explore the site of King Solomon's copper mines. No one has to worry about missing a test or getting off from work for a Jewish holiday. Shabbat is the day stores are closed in Israel and the buses don't run. Israel's calendar meets Jewish religious needs, and being an observant Jew requires no great compromise.

The Nelson Glueck School of Archaeology is part of HUC-JIR's Israel campus. Teams from NFTY and the rabbinical school, among others, have worked on the digs at Gezer, Tel Dan, and the southern wall of the Temple Mount in Jerusalem.

Rabbi Alexander Schindler, president of the UAHC, carries the Torah scroll at a ceremony marking the establishment of Yahel, the first Reform kibbutz in Israel.

This natural integration of religion and everyday life is very appealing, so much so that the Reform movement sends rabbinical students to Israel for their first year at HUC-JIR. The world headquarters of the international Reform movement—the World Union for Progressive Judaism (WUPJ)—is also in Jerusalem.

The special symbol of the Reform Jewish ties to Israel is the first Reform kibbutz, located deep in the Negev. The members of Kibbutz Yahel come from North America, from Reform and Progressive congregations around the world, and from Israel. Day by day they make practical decisions about living their lives in Reform Jewish ways. A second Reform kibbutz, Lotan, has been established in the south and a Reform *mitzpeh* (settlement) called Har Chalutz is being developed in the north.

Reform Jews feel that Reform Judaism can give Israel something it lacks: a way to be religious and modern at the same time. The Reform congregations in Israel offer an alternative to "Orthodoxy or nothing." Many Israelis are secular Jews and reject all religious activities because they associate "religious" with the rigid Orthodoxy which dominates Israeli religious life. Israeli Reform Jews are working to create a contemporary form of Judaism that fits Israeli life. And Israeli-born-and-raised Reform rabbis are becoming the leaders of this movement.

There are as yet very few Israeli Reform congregations. These must fight tooth and nail against the (Orthodox) religious factions in the government for every shred of recognition. The problem is largely political. Israel has been governed since its founding by coalition governments—governments made up of a group of parties, none of which has won a majority by itself in national elections. In order to get the votes it needs to rule, every successful coalition has had to include one or two of the Orthodox religious parties. As the price for their participation, they insist that the Jewish religious activities—which are largely state subsidized—be run according to Orthodox Jewish law.

Moreover, Reform and Conservative rabbis are not officially recognized as rabbis by the Ministry of Religion in Israel. Although the government pays the salaries of rabbis who are officially "recognized"—and the salaries of the Christian and Moslem religious leaders as well—Reform and Conservative rabbis who serve congregations in Israel are not so entitled. Nor can they serve as chaplains in the Israel Defense Forces or perform legally valid marriages or conversions. (See Chapter 5.)

So long as the ruling coalition continues to need the votes of the Orthodox groups in order to stay in power, Israeli Reform Judaism will continue to have problems.

Our Duties to the State of Israel

Reform Jews have certain duties toward the State of Israel. These are not political obligations. Only in our own country are we involved in such things as paying taxes, electing the government, carrying out its laws, and serving in its armed forces.

On the simplest level, good Jews will care very much about what is happening to the State of Israel. They will want to be informed about events there—triumphs and trials alike. Although much of the best Israeli literature is available in translation, many Jews will want to know Hebrew well enough to enjoy the subtle nuances and special flavors of the language. They will surely want to visit Israel from time to time and get to know the country and the people (another good reason for learning the language!). Some North American Jews will decide that they want to work out their Jewish destiny by going to live in the State of Israel.

A vital, effective Jewish state strengthens the Jewish people. Israel's poor and needy, its new immigrants, its underdeveloped neighborhoods, its hand-icapped and aged are our concern too. With Israel's limited means, our help is needed. We must not only provide the financial support (primarily through the United Jewish Appeal) that they cannot supply, but also the cultural activities for which they do not have the necessary funds. American Jews should continue to lend money (through Israel Bonds, for example) for the development of Israeli industry and agriculture or to help begin businesses which have the potential of improving the economic base of the country.

We also have a responsibility at home. We must let our elected repre-

Past and present are fused in this monument by Nathan Rapoport at Kibbutz Yad Mordecai. It commemorates both Mordecai Anilewicz, leader of the Warsaw Ghetto uprising, and the heroic stand of the first settlers of the kibbutz, who were temporarily forced to abandon it during Israel's War of Independence.

The Jews of Israel and the free world helped bring about the *aliyah* of Ethiopian Jews in 1984–1985—another modern miracle.

sentatives know how important the State of Israel is to the long term goals of our own country. It is our job to help our fellow citizens understand the situation of the Israelis, and the degree to which our government's support for Israel helps the security of our country as well. Israel is the only democracy in the Middle East and our most reliable ally. Not too long from now, people your age will be in positions of adult responsibility. If you can help shape their opinions with positive, accurate information you may be making an important contribution to Israel's future—and your own.

Sometimes the Israeli government decides it must do things that some American Jews believe go against Jewish values. What is our obligation then?

It may be that the most difficult and important duty we have to the State of Israel is to love it so much that we will know when we must differ with some of its policies and how we can most usefully and truthfully make our feelings known. In a good family, people not only help and support each other most of the time, but also know when to help through honest, loving (and usually nonpublic) disagreement. That should be our model in our concern for the Land of Israel and our attachment to the State of Israel.

CHAPTER SEVENTEEN

Our Relation to the Jewish Community

There are times in the life of every family when unusual situations occur—a new baby is born, the family moves from one house to another, parents fight, someone gets sick. Unexpected strains are put on everyone's energy and temper. Sometimes the event is a happy one—a Bar/Bat Mitzvah or wedding; sometimes it is a crisis. No matter what the situation, people respond to the challenge in different ways.

Some people decide that whatever is going on doesn't really concern them. Or they complain that what they've been asked to do is too hard. Or they feel that they are not the center of attention and they aren't interested in anyone except themselves. These people want to avoid being involved. They make excuses ("my stomach hurts," "I have too much homework," or "I think I have to go back to the office"), or they disappear when the time comes to be of help, or they stand around criticizing those who do what must be done.

Others do what is assigned to them, feel pleased that they have done their best, and then pay no attention to the rest of the proceedings. Theirs is not a particularly positive attitude either.

Everyone ought to take part in what is going on—advise and encourage those who need it, be proud of family members who succeed in doing their jobs well, support and give aid to those who need physical help. If the occasion is a happy one, part of the "job" is enjoying it; if it is a sad event, then the "job" involves sharing the burden and offering comfort to one another.

The Jewish community also knows those three strategies. Some Jews don't want any part of Judaism. They have "good" excuses for not getting involved or don't care enough even to bother to explain their absence.

Other Jews may pray and study to satisfy themselves yet pay no attention to what the rest of the Jewish community is doing. They aren't interested in what other Jews might need from them or give to them.

Jews who care about the Jewish community are like the members of a family who pull together to cope with every difficult situation and celebrate every happy one. They realize that many things cannot be done alone and that everyone benefits from team effort. This Jewish responsibility begins with participation in a synagogue and extends beyond it to embrace the entire Jewish community.

Identifying the Jewish Community

When we talk about the Jewish "community" we mean many things: the Jews in your neighborhood or with whom your family associates; the members of your synagogue; all the Jews in your town; or all the people served by the agencies in your Federation. We might also have in mind all the Jews in America, or even all the Jews in the world. Despite the many differences of style between East and West, Ashkenazi and Sephardi, Orthodox, Conservative, and Reform, more unites Jews than separates them. They all make up the Jewish community or *k'lal yisrael* (which translates roughly as "the Jewish people").

Reform Jews think of themselves as a loyal, if somewhat daring part of this great Jewish family. They believe that working for the sake of the total Jewish community is an important Reform Jewish obligation.

In a way, we can think of the Jewish community as five bowls "nesting" inside another, each one fitting into the next larger bowl. Innermost, the smallest and first Jewish community you come into is your own family. Through its holiday observances and personal celebrations, its shared memories, its gossip, its dreams and its special way of facing life, you have started to take your place in the Jewish people.

The next "bowl," somewhat larger, is the "extended family" of your congregation. It would certainly be possible to stay at home and carry on your Jewish life in the privacy of your family, but after a while it would probably get very lonely. Imagine what it would be like to have a tutor for all your Ju-

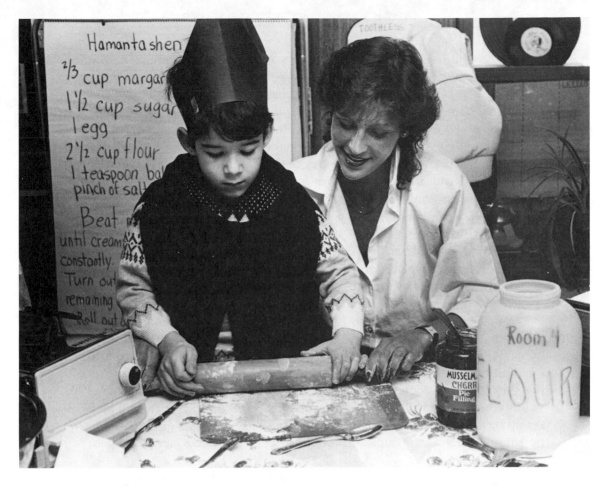

All Jews are members of one community—*k'lal yisrael*—the Jewish people.

daic studies. You might learn as much or more than what you learn in the classroom, but would you want to miss the chance to be with the friends you've made in religious school or the fun you've had together? Having to learn can often mean work, and it's much pleasanter when everyone is doing it together—not to mention the satisfaction that comes from complaining about it later! By contrast, think about the sense you get when you come to services on the High Holidays. The sanctuary is filled, everyone is dressed up, all around you friends and neighbors are welcoming the New Year together. It is a marvelous feeling to be part of a great community celebration.

If you have a local Jewish newspaper, it can also give you something of that feeling. Have you ever looked through its pages to see if you can find the names of your parents or the friends who are active in community organizations? Do you look for your rabbi's name and picture? Or for news of your congregation? If you've walked in a walkathon, or taken part in activities at the YM-YMHA or Jewish Center, or helped out at a telethon, or in special synagogue or youth group events, perhaps you've had the pleasure of finding pictures of yourself in the newspaper as well.

The most space in the newspaper is probably filled with happenings in your local area. Various Jewish family events are recorded—like births, Bar/Bat Mitzvahs, engagements, weddings, and funerals. Social events, synagogue functions, holiday observances, educational opportunities, and organizational meetings are announced. The activities of the communal service agencies that help Jews in your area probably get featured space. All of them are part of what our Jewish "family" is doing.

These Jewish community organizations and agencies are the third "bowl" in the Jewish community "nest." Our communities have created them to meet the great variety of local Jewish needs. They are generally united and perhaps funded through the local Jewish Federation, and often have ties to national groups from which they get help and new ideas.

You can learn a great deal about them by looking at the newspaper.

An article from the Jewish Family Service, for instance, might talk about problems caused by the rising Jewish divorce rate and the difficulties faced by single parent families. The Jewish Vocational Service might have a list of jobs needed for recent immigrants and a notice to potential employers asking that they consider hiring Jewish refugees. There might be requests for volunteers to visit with elderly Jews, either housebound or living in facilities set up by the Federation. (Some communities have "adopt-a-grandparent" type programs that youth groups and religious school students can participate in.)

President Reagan accepts a Prisoner of Conscience bracelet from Stephen Greenberg of the UJA Young Leadership Cabinet. The plight of Soviet Jews is an issue of concern to everyone who cares about human rights and freedom.

The local "Y" or Center probably announces clubs, sports, and cultural activities for youngsters and adults, perhaps featuring special senior citizen programs and vacation day camp plans. And synagogue activities will also be part of this range of activity.

A lot of space in the local Jewish community newspaper is usually given to news of the fund raising appeals that make up much of organized Jewish life. These provide the money for the community's activities, locally and internationally.

There usually is news about what is happening to Jews around the world, with a special focus on the State of Israel. There should be information about national events that affect Jews, and syndicated special features, book and movie reviews, and perhaps sports news and recipes as well. It is remarkable how many different sorts of things we do and are interested in as a Jewish community. It testifies to the liveliness of American Jewish life and enables you personally to contribute to the welfare of Jews in your own community and throughout the world.

Guarding Our Rights

Jewish organizations are also involved with protecting the Jewish community against anti-Semitic activities. Community Relations Councils (CRC) of local UJA Federations, representatives of the Anti-Defamation League (ADL) of B'nai B'rith, the American Jewish Congress, and the American Jewish Committee (AJC) work in this particular area. Perhaps a swastika was painted on the wall of the synagogue or in a school, or there is vandalism, or a fire of suspicious origin takes place in a local Jewish community building. Sometimes Jewish school children are tormented by bullies or made the victims of vicious anti-Jewish jokes. The CRC, ADL or AJC in the local community area will investigate the incident. They want to find out if the activities are serious anti-Semitic attacks or a spur-of-the-moment prank by someone trying to act "smart." Once in a while, a Jewish community gets overly alarmed by an event that would have been best ignored. Occasionally, however, it turns out that seemingly isolated events are part of a pattern going on all over. Then there is cause for serious concern, and the need for broader social and political action.

That is one reason why we need the fourth "bowl" in the Jewish "nest," the national Jewish community. National Jewish organizations in the United States and Canada do the things that we simply can't do on a local level. In the national offices of the CRC, known as the National Jewish Community Relations Advisory Council (NJCRAC), and in the national offices of the ADL, the Congress, and the Committee, trained experts monitor what goes on in every part of our country and around the world. They research the problems and publicize what they think needs public attention. They work behind the scenes with the local Jewish communities, with one another, and with other American groups anxious to protect everyone's civil rights. Together, these national Jewish organizations can help judge the seriousness of a particular incident, exert their influence as nationwide organizations, and give professional advice on how local, state, and national groups should deal with the problem.

Another of our national organizations, located in Washington D.C., is the American Israel Public Affairs Committee (AIPAC). This group of American citizens keeps close watch on United States policy regarding Israel. AIPAC people talk to senators and representatives and try to show them how aiding Israel helps safeguard American foreign policy and the interests of democracy in the Middle East. They publish a newsletter so that individual Jews around the country can also speak intelligently to their neighbors and to their elected representatives in the government on issues related to Israel.

In order to protect the civil rights of Jews (and of all minority groups in America), it is important for many Jews to be knowledgeable about general political affairs. Most of our national organizations make this an important part of their work. Participating in the democratic process is also part of being a good Reform Jew and of safeguarding the Jewish community while working for the benefit of the whole society.

Taking Pride

Many of our most important national institutions are educational and cultural. If you ever visit New York City, be sure to visit the Jewish Museum. There you can see Jewish ritual objects from many centuries, part of the Museum's permanent treasures. Sometimes the Jewish Museum exhibits the work of a modern Jewish painter or sculptor, or features photographs, books, letters, art, and ceremonial Judaica from a Jewish community in another part of the world or from an earlier period of time. There are displays recalling the Holocaust, or explaining how an archeological dig is conducted in Israel. There is also a workshop where resident artists design beautiful modern ritual objects for synagogues and homes—and teach students interested in learning their crafts.

The museum exhibitions help teach everyone, Jewish or not, who comes to see them about the creative talents of our people over the centuries. There are other Jewish museums, of course, and many synagogues have their own display of Jewish art and ritual objects. But in one great national center, very much more can be done. There are many other major Jewish cultural institutions in New York. You will find them listed in the *American Jewish Yearbook*.

We also get a sense of the national Jewish community from the many magazines that deal with Jewish concerns and feature stories and poems of Jewish interest. They bring us into contact with the finest minds and talents among us. The various regional conclaves and national conventions of adult Jewish organizations and youth groups do the same. Getting together with many Jews from nearby towns or from different sections of North America is an exciting experience. Suddenly your personal Jewish community expands. There are opportunities to make new friends, to discover if your problems are unique or shared by others, to find out when you attend services that melodies you love are favorites of Jews all around the country. Meeting that way provides other opportunities as well. It is possible to invite speakers that your local Federation or synagogue or youth group couldn't afford to bring into your own community—specialists in world affairs, or American-Israeli relations, or Bible studies, or famous Jewish writers and artists.

Working together on the national Jewish community level creates a sense of the greatness of the Jewish community and gives the people who participate a feeling of pride in making its extraordinary accomplishments possible.

The World Around Us

The largest "bowl," into which all the others fit, is the community composed of Jews all over the world. Unfortunately, many of our contacts with Jews in foreign countries are limited to our efforts to save them from anti-Semitism. We show our solidarity with Jews in the Soviet Union by wearing prisoner-of-conscience bracelets, by writing letters, and "twinning" with "refuseniks," by protesting to United States and Soviet officials about the way Jews who want to leave the USSR were treated, by marching in demonstrations, by reading special additional prayers at our Passover seders.

Soviet Jews are not the only ones who have suffered. The tiny Jewish communities left in Arab countries remain under great stress. Many Jewish communities in Latin America are threatened by powerful anti-Semitic groups. A remnant of the Ethiopian Jewish community remains trapped in a dreadful situation. We must save these members of our world Jewish community. And we need constantly to be on the alert to help any Jewish group that suddenly finds itself in trouble. For many decades now, the World Jewish Congress, which brings together representatives from localities all over the world, and the UJA, particularly the Joint Distribution Committee, have been the leaders in standing guard for us.

Fortunately, we also have the opportunity to enjoy many positive associations with Jews in other countries. American Jews who tour Jewish sites of interest, particularly in European countries, and who attend synagogue ser-

Left: The couple in the foreground emigrated from the Soviet Union to Israel. When they took a tour of Yad Vashem, the Holocaust memorial in Jerusalem, they were astounded to see their own faces, some thirty years younger, framed in a photograph on the wall. It was taken on the day when their anti-Nazi resistance group was saved by the arrival of the Soviet Army.

Below: Among the last remaining Jews of Cracow, Poland were Cantor and Mrs. Fogel, who took care of the Remu Synagogue. It was built by the great sixteenth century rabbi and scholar, Moses Isserles.

A haunting feature of the Scuola Canton, an old synagogue in the ghetto of Venice, is its sukkah. The sukkah still contains remnants of the last Sukkot celebrated there, just before the Venetian Jews were deported to concentration camps.

vices in the foreign cities they are visiting, often receive a warm welcome. They come back with stories about having made new, good friends or even of being invited home for Shabbat dinner by one of the worshipers. Some have walked into a synagogue while a wedding or Bar Mitzvah was taking place and found themselves treated as guests of honor, "cousins" from America, simply because they are fellow Jews. People who have had such experiences will tell you how surprised they were to suddenly realize what deep Jewish ties they shared with these strangers into whose lives they have been welcomed.

Our religion is more than a personal, a family or a synagogue matter. It calls for each of us to contribute to the proud survival of our people as a whole—and thus, to the fulfillment of its ongoing relationship with God. So Jews who care will be involved in the Jewish community, from the local to the international level. They will contribute time, energy, ideas, and money to the organizations whose specific causes need their help.

Is that a lot to ask of you as you grow into a Jewish adult? Perhaps. But it is what caring Jews have always done and now it is our turn to do the same.

CHAPTER EIGHTEEN

Reaching Out to Our Country and the World

T he first Jews came to North America in September, 1654. The follow-ing year, one of them—Asser Levy—fought an important battle against the authorities, a fight to make Jews equal citizens. The governor of New Amsterdam ordered all citizens to serve in the militia—except the Jews, who were to pay a tax instead. Asser Levy understood that this was discrimination. He knew that unless Jews shared the obligations of their fellow citizens they could never be their equals. So he fought for and won the right to bear arms.

Had Asser Levy and the hundreds of thousands of Jews who came here later not taken full civic responsibility we would not have the equality we do today.

The history of Reform Judaism is tied up with the struggle of Jews to de-termine their Jewish obligations in democratic societies. Unfortunately, tra-ditional Judaism seemed to offer little guidance in this area because for nearly fifteen hundred years Jews hadn't been allowed to participate as equals in so-ciety. But the early Reform rabbis quickly identified the Jewish teachings that could guide them: there is one God for all people; we are all one human family; we must observe a single standard of justice and mercy for everyone; peace and understanding must be the same goal for all; we must have special

Uriah Phillips Levy (1792—1862) ran away to sea at the age of ten. He rose to the rank of Commodore, the highest then possible in the United States Navy. One of his most important accomplishments was the abolishment of flogging, a brutal form of punishment common at that time. Today there is a Jewish chapel named after him at the Naval Station in Norfolk, Virginia.

Jonas Phillips received this two-dollar certificate for services to the Continental Army. He did not cash it, he later said, because he did not desire pay for helping a cause as just as the American Revolution.

During the First World War, in an improvised chapel in Paris, France, American soldiers joined together to celebrate the High Holy Days.

Rabbi Bertram W. Korn was appointed admiral in the United States Navy, the highest rank ever attained by a Jewish chaplain. Helping Rabbi Korn's mother is the then Chief of Chaplains, Father John J. O'Connor, now Cardinal of New York.

concern for the quality of everyday life. These teachings say that Jews have duties to everyone—they are *universal* ethics.

The New "Commandments" that Came with Democracy

Civic duties are sometimes difficult obligations that demand responsible action. Serving in the armed forces is one such duty and American Jews have fought in every United States war. They have been honored for heroism in high proportion to their small numbers. (Yet the Jewish commitment to peace is so strong that some believing Jews have, with the support of the rest of the community, made pacifism the core of their ethics.)

The right to vote is perhaps the greatest privilege of living in a functioning democracy. (Imagine what it must be like to live in a country where only a military coup or revolution can change the government!) Every concerned citizen ought to be familiar with local, state and national affairs and then vote whenever there is an election.

Often, special issues appear on the ballot, requiring voters to decide how tax money should be spent. People vote "yes" or "no" on questions like whether or not to provide housing for the elderly or build a new road or increase salaries for public school teachers, police, or firefighters. In a democracy, every citizen can help decide the right course of action.

Elections are the most dramatic part of the democratic process. Between elections the work of the parties needs to be carried on. Issues must be studied, personnel scrutinized, funds raised, and preparations made for the next election. People who have worked to elect a candidate should feel an obligation to monitor their candidate's performance in office. Is he/she living up to campaign promises? Paying attention to voters' concerns? Responding to new—or forgotten—issues?

How Much Leadership Should Government Exercise?

The biggest sacrifice—of time, energy, and money—is made by those who are willing to serve in government posts. Certainly, some become famous or have a good deal of power. Most, however, aren't very well known to the average citizen. People who run for office must accept a great deal of abuse from their opponents—not only before they are elected but during the whole time they hold that position. They have very little time for family life. In addition, they generally earn far less money in government than they could be making in private business. It is easy to see why some officials are tempted to steal—and why the honesty and competence of the overwhelming majority of officeholders is one of the glories of our democracy.

Jews have eagerly responded to the responsibilities of democracy. A large percentage regularly exercise their right to vote. Over the years, many Jews have run for political office or have otherwise been very active in political affairs. All of these activities are part of what Reform Judaism understands as universal ethics.

Until fairly recently, the rights stated in the Declaration of Independence and the Constitution of the United States were far more idealistic than the actual practices of different parts of the country—or, in fact, of the nation as a whole. In order to have the laws apply equally to all citizens, the national government took matters into its own hands, passed new, stronger laws and enforced them. The child labor laws prohibiting the employment of youngsters in factories and mines, the laws calling for the elimination of dangerous and unsanitary working conditions, and the laws demanding equality for minority groups are three of the many such ethical enactments. Many Jews have been pleased by government intervention in such issues because they have seen it as a reasonable and effective way to help create the ethical society Judaism envisions.

The *universal* ethics of Reform Judaism include involvement in the democratic processes of our country's political life. Former Senator Rudy Boschwitz of Minnesota exemplifies this ideal.

In recent years, however, there has been considerable argument among Jews (as among other Americans) about what the government's role should be in such matters and where its efforts might cause as much harm as help. Obviously, determining how the political process can help us achieve our ethical values is very complicated. Devoted Jews will therefore give such questions most serious attention.

Bettering Things Outside the Political Process

However, the political process is not enough. An extraordinary range of volunteer activities helps to improve the quality of life in America. From the earliest years of its independence, visitors to the United States were surprised at how much time most Americans seemed to spend doing good for other people. Possibly this came about because the pioneers needed to count on one another for help.

When Jews came to America they found the pattern of volunteer activity very familiar for they had always established volunteer *hevrot* for causes like caring for the sick, providing dowries for poor young women, or rescuing Jews from slavery. Not surprisingly, Jews have become involved in every secular community activity that has not discriminated against their participation. They have been enthusiastic supporters of all sorts of movements for human development, education, and culture.

Even in a democracy, people who are rich or have social influence have special ethical opportunities. Success too often makes people think only of themselves, their present pleasures, and their future gains. They lose sight of the fact that others continue to face hardships and to operate with the kind of handicaps that cannot be overcome alone. Jewish ethics remind us that the greater people are the more they can and ought to do for others. Elected officials and other opinion makers, too, are more likely to respond to the suggestions of important people than they are to those of ordinary citizens. If you become wealthy or famous or influential some day, will you remember to try to improve life for everyone? Will you fight snobbery and prejudice in your clubs and associations, and stand up for the needy and the powerless? Judaism doesn't want *martyrs* for ethical progress—but all of us now or later should use our influence for the universal good.

Our ethical obligations extend to the world as a whole. This is most evident when disaster strikes and major relief efforts are immediately launched to help the victims of hurricanes, earthquakes, volcanos or floods. Ethical obligations are less obvious with the "normal" problems like disease, hunger, illiteracy, lack of human rights and, above all, war and the threat of war.

How difficult it is for us to be of help. We have so little power—and the international organizations that are charged with global ethical concerns either seem not to have the power to correct inequities, or else choose not to exercise their power in fair or constructive ways. But no matter how complex and perplexing the situation seems, we must never stop trying to apply our ethical standards to the world as a whole.

Universal Ethics as a Challenge

Some Jews disagree. They argue that our primary Jewish obligations are to Jews, not to non-Jewish society. They make two important points. They argue, first, that it is a bad idea for practical reasons—the greater the social problem the less we seem able to accomplish (and the more likely we are to be criticized for our efforts). Second, they also insist that a group as little and as threatened as the Jewish community should be concentrating its energies on its own survival; Jewish social ethics, they say, ought to be directed mainly to Jews.

The teachers of Reform Judaism have not agreed. When Jews were isolated by the rest of humankind, our sages wisely focused our ethical duties on our own people—but never limited them only to Jews. Judaism is not a religion only about Jews but about Jews as part of the human family. Now that we are increasingly becoming complete partners in the fate of our society and the world, the neglected part of Jewish duty must come into its own.

True, we have known bitter—indeed, unparalleled—suffering in recent decades. But that does not change the facts: we do not live in ghettos, culturally or physically segregated. The Emancipation made it possible for us to live radically better lives than anyone had ever imagined. And like our ancestors, our modern move from slavery to freedom ought to give us an enlarged sense of Jewish responsibility.

A Light to the Nations

Some generations back, Reform rabbis gave a name to their sense of global ethical purpose. They called it the "Mission of Israel." They were going to teach ethical monotheism to all humankind. They felt that no other faith taught ethical religion so clearly, and that it was therefore the obligation of modern Jews to share this insight with the world.

For many years, the power of this idea inspired many Jews to lives of high idealism. The astonishing record of modern Jewish ethical accomplishment in almost every aspect of human service is testimony to the strength of this ideal. Even those modernized Jews who spurned Judaism and used politics

Henry Kissinger, advisor to Presidents and a winner of the Nobel Prize for Peace, addresses the General Assembly of the Council of Jewish Federations.

to correct the evils of society claimed that this was the realistic way to reach humanity's messianic goal! (How these Socialists and Marxists were often duped by their groups is a sad story indeed.)

Few Reform rabbis still preach the Mission of Israel. Modern reality has been very harsh on idealistic dreams. Good people once hoped that the existence of a world forum would bring world peace—and now the United Nations has become the home of the vilest political hypocrisy. The truth seems to be that human nature does not become ethical simply through education or culture—the Nazis taught us that all too well. Nor is the fact that people live in a democracy in itself a safeguard: even in our own country we have seen intelligent, thoughtful people become corrupt and sinful.

Besides, the Jews have no monopoly on ethics. We share many of our universal ideals with other liberals. Our mission to improve the world is one we share with all concerned human beings.

There is also something wrong about saying that the only purpose of Judaism is to serve the world. No one lives primarily for other people. Being Jewish is wonderful for itself and doesn't need to be justified by its "mission" to non-Jews. That, however, does not mean we have duties only to other Jews.

Why Particularism Alone is Wrong

Imagine what would happen if the American Jewish community made the following public announcement: "Jews have suffered so much over the centuries because of non-Jews that we owe you no more than the barest minimum support. We need every bit of our own strength for ourselves. We will take what we can from America, both for ourselves and for the State of Israel—but don't look to us for any real contribution to this country. We aren't interested in helping any society but our own."

How do you think our fellow citizens would react? Chances are they would consider us unethical and refuse to have much to do with us. People who act selfishly can count on others to act selfishly to them.

We Jews cannot survive alone. Even practically, we have a stake in social betterment. When social ills grow, people look for scapegoats and have often vented their frustration on Jews. Therefore, we need to alleviate hardship where we can and protect every minority's safety. By so doing, we protect our own. The same is true globally. Environmental pollution, the depletion of natural resources or nuclear disaster will not selectively spare Jews, Jewish neighborhoods, or the Jewish state. In everyday fact, as in Jewish ideals, humankind is one and needs to live by that understanding.

We need to strike a balance. It would be as wrong to only serve humanity as it would be to focus exclusively on Judaism. Simple self-respect makes it plain that the first level of Jewish duty is to Jews. Who will work for our needs and fight for our goals if not we ourselves? "If I am not for myself, who will be for me?" But since Jews are now part of society and belong to the global community, we need to give an important part of our energies to general human concerns. "If I am only for myself, what kind of person am I?" A mature Jewish religious life demands concern for ourselves and others—particularism and universalism—and requires action in behalf of both. "If not now, when?"

PART FIVE

In Closing

How easy it is to get disappointed. You look forward to going some where or getting something and then it doesn't happen. It can make you feel very bad. If what you wanted was very important to you or if someone you had always trusted failed you, the sadness can be overwhelming. Everyone has had that experience. Learning not to be defeated by disappointments but finding the courage to go on, slowly and painfully if necessary, is a major part of growing up. We all admire people who rebuild their lives after a great blow. We also know that people who stay dejected for a long time need special help and attention.

Judaism has always, despite the great suffering and hardship experienced by Jews across the centuries, had faith and hope in a better future. It has helped Jews go on, and it has helped direct the ethical focus of their lives. Reform Judaism made some changes in the ideas about how this hope would be realized—but the basic concept has remained the same for hundreds and hundreds of years.

In this final chapter, we will discuss the nature of Jewish hope and why it is so important for all of us.

CHAPTER NINETEEN

Our Hope for the Messianic Age

You would think that with all the persecution Jews have faced, Judaism would teach a sour view of life and encourage Jews to be pessimists. On the contrary. When Jews complain, when Jews express a strong sense of things not being right, it is not because they hate life but because they have such high ideals. Criticism seems to be a way of living with the disappointment of unrealized hopes. Ours is a religion of great hope.

We want to conclude our study of Reform Judaism with this important lesson.

The Traditional Vision of the Messiah

Jewish hope, so often frustrated in everyday life, was very early linked to the idea of the Messiah. The word *messiah* comes from the Hebrew root for dabbing or smearing with oil. In the days before soap or medicines, various oils were used for cleansing, healing, cooling, and covering unpleasant odors. Part of the ceremony of installing a priest or a king involved dabbing that person with a special oil—the official was *anointed* (literally, rubbed with oil). By the time of the Rabbis, the hoped-for perfect king who would solve all the ills of the world became known as *the* anointed one, the *mashiah*—in English, Messiah.

The Messiah was understood to be human, a decendant of King David. During periods of great Jewish suffering, rumors of the arrival of the Messiah and followers of self-declared Messiahs could be found even among educated and influential people. The great Rabbi Akiba announced (probably in the year 135 C.E.) that Simon Bar Kochba was the Messiah. In later centuries, when Jews were suffering and endangered, a number of "false" messiahs attracted Jewish followers. Gluckel of Hameln (who lived from 1646 to 1724) records in her diary her personal recollections of how the false messiah Sabbatai Zevi affected her family's life: "Many people sold home, hearth and everything they possessed, awaiting redemption. My father-in-law (a wealthy businessman), peace unto him, who lived in Hameln, moved from there, leaving things standing in the house, just as they were. . . . He sent us here, to Hamburg, two big barrels of linenware, in them were all kinds of food—peas, smoked meat, all sorts of dried fruits—that could keep without going bad. The good man thought they would leave from Hamburg for the Holy Land. These barrels were more than a year in my house. At last, fearing that the meat and other things would get spoilt, he wrote that we should open the barrels and take out all the food, so that the linen underneath should not spoil. They remained here for three more years, my father-in-law always expecting to need them at a moment's notice for his journey."

How could a human being accomplish such miracles or be a "perfect" king? With God's special help said the Jewish Sages. Then God's rule would be as real on earth as it is now only "in heaven." So another way of talking about the great Jewish hope was to refer to the coming of God's Kingdom— but no *person* is involved in this notion.

These two sides of the Messiah idea—the human and the Godly—showed up in different ways in different thinkers. People were free to imagine whatever details they wished. As a result, the range of Jewish messianic speculation over the centuries has been incredibly varied.

The Conflict with Christianity

If you have ever been approached by a Christian missionary, you may be surprised that we have not quoted any Bible verses to illustrate Jewish ideas about the Messiah. The reason is simple: scholars today simply cannot agree on how much, if any, of Judaism's classic notion of the Messiah comes from the Bible. Some say that the passages that seem to contain the origins of this belief are really only expressions of the biblical writer's longing for a better government or a decent life. Others argue that the basic theme of God helping history come to a sacred conclusion through the person of a perfect king is already present in various biblical texts. They agree only that the vision of the Messiah was more fully developed in rabbinic times.

What complicates the discussion is the centuries-old argument between Christians and Jews over whether or not the Bible *predicts* the coming of a Messiah and whether or not a certain Jew, Joshua (Jesus), from the town of Nazareth had fulfilled the prophets' "predictions." If you read the accounts of Jesus' life as given in the books of Matthew, Mark and Luke in the Christian Bible, you will see that while the three accounts do not agree with one another in many important details, they all use quotations from the Jewish Bible to prove that Jesus was the expected Anointed One. In their eagerness to support their belief, they—and later Christians as well—found many texts which they interpreted as predictions of Jesus the Messiah (Christ means messiah in Greek). These are the texts still being quoted by Christians who want to convert Jews to Christianity.

Over the centuries, Jews have had little difficulty rejecting the Christian claims. Jewish scholars have pointed to the many cases where people who didn't know Hebrew had read the Bible in translation and simply misapplied it. The most famous example is that of the "virgin" birth—the report that Jesus was the child of a mother, Miriam (Mary), who remained a virgin. The supporting passage appears in Chapter 7, verse 14 of the Book of Isaiah. To begin with, Jews do not see anything "messianic" about the passage itself. More important, the Hebrew does not say "virgin" but "young woman." Many

This *wimpel,* or binder around the Torah, is from Trinidad, Colorado. It shows its creator's pride in being both Jewish and American.

Christians today accept this correction. Even an "official" Protestant translation of the Bible, the Revised Standard Version, now follows the Hebrew properly.

Another example is Second Isaiah's poem about the "suffering servant" in Chapter 53. There certainly seems to be some correspondence between the way Christians describe Jesus and what the Hebrew says. However—and it is a big however—such "hints" and "predictions" are completely foreign to the Hebrew Bible. Jewish scholars point out that much more *disagrees* with the identification than supports it. The servant should more properly be identified either as the Jewish people or as the prophet Isaiah himself.

Liberal Jews have added two other arguments. Believing as we do that religion is mainly human, we argue that Christian Scripture, like Jewish Scripture, was written by people. The early Christians, very likely unconsciously, shaped their stories of Jesus to fit what they knew from the Bible (the Hebrew one, that is—they were in the process of creating the Christian Bible.) The language of the Bible helped them explain and prove their belief. Later generations accepted the various disciples' accounts as truth (despite the fact that they don't tell identical stories), and pious Christians still take them as such. We think that the Gospels say more about the faith of the people who wrote them than about what actually happened.

Most convincing to all Jews was the unfortunate evidence: If the Messiah had come, why was the world still so evil? If the Messiah was supposed to bring justice and harmony, where were they? There can be argument about the meaning of verses in the Bible, but everyone seems to agree that our world still needs radical improvement.

The Christians say that Jesus came to earth the first time to explain what the Messiah would be really like: he would not be a conquering king at all but a humble servant who would die for human sins even though he was innocent of them and would thereby gain God's forgiveness for all humankind. Early Christians believed that when Jesus finally returned, only those people who already believed in him would be welcome in God's Kingdom.

Jews see no hint of this double coming in the words of the Jewish prophets. Nor have we seen any evidence of change in human behavior since the first coming. Jewish suffering over the centuries has seemed to us an irrefutable argument against Christian claims.

Reform Jews Rethink the Messiah Idea

Christian ideas of the Messiah were unacceptable. But even the old Jewish symbol of the Messiah as king no longer seemed logical to many Jews in the post-ghetto world.

In the first place, it was too political. When the Messiah "arrived," Jews would all leave the countries where they lived—and were now citizens—and become subjects of their own king in the Land of Israel. Of course, the idea was largely symbolic—but it no longer appealed to people who had finally gained citizenship.

Secondly, a belief in the miraculous return of all Jews—living and dead—to the Land of Israel was very unscientific. The notion of the resurrection of the dead (dead bodies being reconstituted, perfected, and given new life) was as unacceptable as the notion that humans and nature could be suddenly transformed into another state of being.

The early Reformers thought that they had a much better way of expressing their Jewish hope. They saw that democracy and political action were bringing more benefits than prayers for the Messiah had ever done. So they looked to humanity to change itself: If ignorance, superstition, thoughtless habit and self-serving power were what stood in the way of true peace, then if only everyone were educated, they might join one another to transform the world. Instead of longing for the King Messiah, they now concentrated on the perfect era that the Messiah was supposed to usher in. They called that fulfilled world the Messianic Age and believed that all people, Jews and non-Jews alike, were responsible for making it a reality.

Nor did the Messianic Age seem like a far off, impossibly distant ideal for Reform Jews during the first half of the twentieth century. When science discovered new truths about human life, when technology improved the way people lived, when democracy was extended to additional groups and classes, they saw the Messianic Age being built around them.

This vision was so attractive to them that it influenced their lives in two significant ways. First, because they identified the goal of Judaism with improving the world, they joined in every effort to right social wrongs and make life more humane. Even Jews who had little connection with Judaism were powerfully moved by the impulse to achieve greater justice and mercy.

Second, it gave special purpose to being Jewish. The Jewish people could serve all humanity by teaching others what they had now learned—that all people were not only children of one God, but that they could bring God's Kingdom into being by working together. They saw it as the unique Mission of Israel to live this message and to teach it to everyone.

Becoming More Realistic About Human Nature

By the second half of the twentieth century, it became increasingly difficult for Reform Jews to retain their old messianic optimism. Better education, increased employment and the spread of culture have not made people highly

Acts of prejudice can still occur in our country. When a synagogue was defaced in New Jersey, Governor Thomas Kean shared the outrage of the Jewish community and helped wipe off the anti-Semitic graffiti.

ethical. Indeed, it seems that there is deceit and crookedness almost everywhere one looks—in government, industry, sports, the arts. It is difficult for idealistic people not to be disillusioned.

The Jewish community has suffered the special pain of the Holocaust. Our people were slaughtered not by lunatics on a rampage but by a nation whose people were among the best educated and most cultured in the world. Its leaders could enlist large numbers of ordinary people to simply follow orders, even though the "orders" turned them into methodical murderers of innocent men, women, and children. And the bystanders who knew what was going on, did not protest or try to stop them—and we now know that included the Western democracies, among them our own country.

The continuing power of anti-Semitism, despite the growth of democracy, echoes the lessons of the Holocaust. In the Soviet Union, to mention only the most dramatic case, Jews have been oppressed in new ways that, nevertheless, open historic Jewish wounds. Even in the United States, the greatest exemplar of freedom and pluralism, anti-Semitism has become more open and less unthinkable than we had previously believed.

Many people have begun to lose faith in humankind's ability to truly better the world. Some rush off to find a cult to save them; others look for a drug that will keep them from facing reality. A terrifying number of teenagers commit suicide and too many husbands and wives refuse to try to learn how to deal with one another. Can anyone then believe that people can create the Messianic Age on their own?

Yes, people have great limitations and society regularly disappoints us, but we Jews have not given up our messianic hope. Astonishingly, a major source of our continuing trust has been the Holocaust, the source of so much pain.

"We Therefore Hope O Eternal One, Our God, Soon to Behold . . ."

Some Jews in Nazi death camps felt so completely betrayed by everything that they had believed in that they gave up on life and lived like robots. Their fellow inmates (for reasons no one remembers) called them "Musselmen." But they were the exception. Why did most of the Jews in the camps not become "Musselmen" too? Incredible as it seems, even in the death camps some Jews managed acts of spiritual heroism and physical resistance. They fought back against everything that the murderers stood for with some life-affirming act, some Jewish religious celebration, some humanitarian deed.

And the way the survivors—and their children and grandchildren—have carried on since World War II has been no less amazing. They refused to give up on life. They started over again—they married, had children, made plans for the future, and slowly but resolutely began to take their places in the world. Their refusal to despair is in itself one of the greatest human and Jewish achievements of all time. Their lives say that the worst evil need not have the final say in human affairs, and that goodness, though it may seem weak in comparison, has a power that should never be underestimated.

When we are dejected by what we see around us or feel going on inside us, we should remember what they overcame. It is an indication of what we too are capable of doing.

Something similar may be said of the accomplishments of the State of Israel. Bringing the State of Israel into existence was an act of supreme ethical defiance. Its continuing concern for human values, despite all the problems the Israelis face, has made Jews the world over proud of their people. We can

Rabbi Eugene B. Borowitz shares a special moment of understanding with his daughter. When we listen to one another, when we feel love, we have a sense of God within us and we know we are not alone.

take courage from the Israelis' refusal to be destroyed by their problems. We can be inspired by their unconquerable will.

These great examples—and countless smaller ones—have rekindled the old Jewish faith that God, too, has a part in bringing the Messianic Age. We do not understand why there is so much evil in the world or why it is so difficult to bring humankind to righteousness. We do not know why God's "help" does not come faster or more effectively. But we did not have to give up our modern ideas of God because of the Holocaust. What changed was our modern estimate of humankind. In our optimistic years we believed that we, simply by self-improvement, could all be the Messiah. The Holocaust and all the other disillusioning events of our time have made it brutally clear that we are not that smart. Certainly humankind can wipe out much of the evil around them, and there is no excuse for our not doing what we can. But we have our limits. As Judaism has always taught, we are partners with God in this great task. God guides our power to do good. When we have done our best and evil still abounds, we must rely on God's own staying power to see that righteousness eventually triumphs. We may momentarily be defeated—but God's goodness remains supreme. That is the ultimate source of our Jewish Hope and determination.

We hope you will remember that in your own life. We want you to join us, the Jewish people and decent human beings everywhere, in trying to bring justice and peace to the world.

And when your disappointments and failures sometimes seem overwhelming, remember the teaching of your tradition. No matter what you have done or what has happened to you, you are not alone and rejected. God never gives up on people; God will never let you go. God remains your personal partner just as God is now, as in the past, the partner of the people of Israel. Build your relationship with God and with the people of Israel. Through it you will gain one of Judaism's most valued gifts, the courage to live nobly—and to live with hope.

Index

PHOTO CREDITS

American Jewish Archives: Pages 11, 19, 20, 25, 26, 96, 97, 135, 147. American Jewish Historical Society: Pages 18, 71, 161 (bottom). Art Resource: Pages 85, 87. Beth Hatfutzot: Page 59 (left). Bnai Yehuda Synagogue, Kansas City, Mo. Pages 76 (left); 93. E.B. Borowitz: Page 120. C.C.A.R.: Page 137 (top). Robert A. Cumins: Pages 154, 164, 167. Frank Darmstaedter: Page 114. Harvey Finkel: Page 144. Abraham Freedman: Page 117. H.U.C.-J.I.R.: Pages 37, 78, 102, 121, 132 (bottom), 146. E.J. Hockley: Page 33 (left). H.U.C. Skirball Museum: Page 30 (top), 33, 172. Jewish Community Council, Tucson, Az.: Page 69. Jewish Museum: Page 32. Jewish Welfare Board: Pages 125, 162 (top). Joods Historisch Museum, Amsterdam, Holland: Page 36. Robert L. Kern: Pages 41 (top left), 128. Leo Baeck Institute: Pages 3, 8, 13, 15, 60 (bottom), 132 (top). Jane Linden: Page 126. Richard Lobel: Page 150. National Religious Press: Page 44. New Jersey Newsphotos: Page 175. Norman R. Patz: Pages 44, 148, 158 (bottom), 159. Stanley K. Patz: 60 (top), 95, 137 (bottom). Federation of Jewish Agencies of Greater Philadelphia: Pages 123 (top), 142, 153. Keneseth Israel, Philadelphia, Pa. Page 162. Ramaz School: Page 41, Nathan Rapoport: Page 149. Allan Reider: Pages 42, 59 (right), 107 (bottom). Religious News Service: Page 177. Alfred Rubens: Page 5. Rabbi Laurence H. Rubinstein: Pages 60 (top), 117. Spanish Portuguese Synagogue, New York, N.Y.: Page 41 (bottom). Temple Oheb Shalom, Baltimore, Md.: Pages 72 (top), 95. Temple Sholom of West Essex, Cedar Grove, N.J.: Pages 62, 64, 72, 103, 107 (top). United Jewish Appeal: Pages 46, 91. United States Naval Institute: Page 161 (top). Walters Art Gallery: Page 86. Fani Weissman: Page 158 (top). U.A.H.C.: Pages 4, 22, 30 (bottom), 31, 34, 52, 54, 74, 77, 88, 104, 108. U.A.H.C. Camp Harlam: Page 123.